James D Bratt

Seasonable
Revolutionary

Seasonable Revolutionary

THE MIND OF CHARLES CHAUNCY

Charles H. Lippy

Nelson-Hall nh Chicago

LIBRARY OF CONGRESS CATALOGING IN PUBLICATION DATA

Lippy, Charles H.
Seasonable revolutionary.

Bibliography: p.
Includes index.
1. Chauncy, Charles, 1705–1787. 2. Congregational churches—Clergy—Biography. 3. Clergy—Massachusetts—Boston—Biography. 4. Boston (Mass.)—Biography. I. Title.
BX7260.C527L56 285.8'32'0924 [B] 81-9560
ISBN 0-88229-625-6 AACR2

Manufactured in the United States of America

10 9 8 7 6 5 4 3 2 1

For my parents,
Charles A. and Natalie S. Lippy

Contents

Preface

Some years ago in a graduate seminar on Jonathan Edwards taught by Professor Lefferts A. Loetscher of the Princeton Theological Seminary, the figure of Charles Chauncy, Edwards's primary opponent, attracted my attention. As I probed the literature of the Great Awakening, I found references to Chauncy and his writings in abundance. Yet there was no scholarly monograph in print which examined his life and thought. I determined later to pursue this Puritan preacher to find out precisely what he had to say. I quickly discovered that he was "the most influential minister of his time in Boston."[1] Tory Peter Oliver, Chauncy's political foe, grudgingly acknowledged Chauncy to be "Head Master of the School of the Prophets."[2] My initial study of Chauncy took the form of a doctoral dissertation submitted to the Department of Religion of Princeton University. One section of that dissertation became the nucleus for this intellectual biography.

I remain convinced that Chauncy is a man deserving of further analysis. Because his life spanned the greater part of the eighteenth century (1705–1787) and because he was involved in most of the religious and political turmoil of that age from the Great Awakening to the War for Independence, Chauncy and his work offer the historian ready materials for increasing our knowledge of the later colonial period. As the text will demonstrate, his impact extended to virtually every dimension of life in eighteenth century Massachusetts. Chauncy was a cantankerous, combative sort, always ready to engage in controversy, relentlessly driving home his points, and never publicly doubting the validity of his views. Even after living with him through his writings for a decade now, I have not developed a deep affection for his character. Chauncy did not readily receive the love even of his peers. But he did receive and deserve their respect, and he merits our attention. I have acquired an enduring appreciation for the substantial contribution he made to American life and thought and commend him to other students of early American culture.

As is always the case in scholarly research, the preparation of this study brought opportunities to explore rare book and manuscript holdings at several libraries. For permitting access to materials and, in many cases, for providing places to think and work, I wish to express appreciation to the following libraries and societies and their staffs: the American Academy of Arts and Sciences; the American Philosophical Association; the Beinecke Library, Yale University; the Boston Public Library; the William L. Clements Library, University of Michigan; the Harvard University Archives; the Historical Society of Pennsylvania; the Houghton and Widener Libraries, Harvard University; the Library of Congress; the Long Island Historical Society; the Massachusetts Historical Society; the National Archives and Records Service; the New York Public Library; the Speer Library, Princeton Theological Seminary; the library of the Union Theological Seminary, New York City; the University of Pennsylvania; and, most especially, the Firestone Library, Princeton University. Thanks also to Mrs. Donald Hyde, owner of the R. B. Adam Collection. I am likewise grateful to Oberlin College for released time during the Winter Term of 1974 which provided an opportunity for the initial rewriting of several sections of the manuscript. A Summer Stipend from the National Endowment for the Humanities in 1975 allowed me to conduct the research for Chapter Five concerning the relationship between Chauncy and Richard Price. The typing of the final draft was made possible by a grant from the Clemson University Faculty Research Committee.

A word of gratitude is also due many persons who assisted me in multitudinous ways in my work. Professors John F. Wilson, Horton Davies, and Paul Ramsey of the Department of Religion and Professor Emeritus Wesley Frank Craven of the Department of History, Princeton University, offered valuable counsel at various stages of research and writing, and Professor Emeritus Clyde A. Holbrook, Oberlin College, commented on a preliminary draft of Chapter

Two. Mrs. Betty Barrett graciously and most carefully typed the final draft. But my greatest debt is to my valued associate and friend, Professor Catherine L. Albanese of Wright State University. Professor Albanese painstakingly read the completed manuscript and provided such judicious criticisms that the work would be naught without the changes she suggested. Of course, I remain solely responsible for any errors of fact and for the interpretation of the life and thought of Charles Chauncy offered.

Thanks must also be extended to several journals for permission to include in this work materials which appeared in their pages in another form. Some material from chapter 2 appeared as "The Great Awakening: an Opponent's Perspective," *Ohio Journal of Religious Studies,* 2:1 (1974): 44–52, copyright 1974 by Cleveland State University. Material in chapter 5 was utilized in "Restoring a Lost Ideal: Charles Chauncy and the American Revolution," *Religion in Life,* 44 (1975): 491–502, copyright 1975 by Abingdon Press, and in "Trans-Atlantic Dissent and the Revolution: Richard Price and Charles Chauncy," *Eighteenth Century Life,* 4:2 (1977): 31–37, copyright 1977 by the University of Pittsburgh.

1.

Portrait of a Preacher

Charles Chauncy
Born in Boston, January, 1705
Great Grandson of Charles Chauncy
President of Harvard College
Graduated at Harvard College 1721
Minister of this Church 1727–1787
Doctor of Divinity 1742 University of Edinburgh
Died in Boston 10 Febr 1787
A Founder of the American Academy of
Arts and Sciences
Defender of Liberal Congregationalism
Writer of learned and influential Treatises
Rational Dispassionate Intrepid
Scornful of Extravagance and Pretense
He guided his Generation to
Political and Religious
Freedom

This inscription, from a plaque placed on the north wall of Boston's First Church in 1917 by the descendants of Charles Chauncy, capsules the life of one of early America's most eminent clergymen. Settled at the prominent parish in 1727, Chauncy ministered in that era when the United States was forged in the crucible of Britain's colonial empire. It was an age when the tenuous religious bonds which had shaped the Puritan immigrants to New England were finally and irrevocably shattered. And it was a time when a religiously pluralistic culture emerged from the fires of controversy—over the Great Awakening, over the proposed establishment of an American Anglican episcopate, and over the remolding of orthodox theology in a rationalistic cast.

In all these movements the First Church divine had a hand. And as the century wore on, more and more Chauncy came to epitomize, symbolize, and indeed speak for that curious breed of persons who wished to remain faithful to the heritage of the past as they understood it, while reinterpreting it in fresh ways to serve future generations.

Chauncy passed the first several years of his active ministry without attracting unusual public attention. Most likely, his time was spent fulfilling the traditional duties of the New England Puritan cleric: long hours in the study poring over the Scriptures and preparing sermons; visiting the sick, the bereaved, and those in need of spiritual counsel; preaching the Word in the meetinghouse; instructing men and women of all ages in matters concerning the ultimate destiny of their souls. If it was not a sparkling existence, it at least carried with it the respect and authority due one who guided persons in the all-important ways of salvation and godliness. Indeed, religious concerns had so long permeated Puritan New England that the clergyman had become not simply a minister of the gospel, but the symbol of a style, of the Puritan social order, of the history of those now of the past whose lives and ideas shaped the present and would give birth to the future. Heir to this tradition, Chauncy embarked upon a ministerial career. But there was little in his early life to suggest that he would be catapulted to fame when the evangelical revivals swept across New England in the opening years of the 1740s and never be far from the public eye until his death in 1787.

The Chauncy family had been part of the Massachusetts

enterprise almost from its inception. The great-grandfather of the First Church pastor, also named Charles, brought his family to join the "errand into the wilderness" in 1638.[1] An Anglican priest of distinctly Puritan sympathies, Chauncy had fallen victim to the drive for absolute conformity to official Church of England practice propelled by the zealous Archbishop William Laud. The issue in Chauncy's case seems trivial in retrospect, yet at the time it symbolized not only the widening rift between conformists and dissenters, but the conflict between opposing religious styles—Anglican and Puritan. The pastor in the parish of Ware refused to comply with the ecclesiastical directive to read the Book of Sports to his flock. Regarded by the establishment as enjoining healthy celebration of the created order, the Book of Sports, first issued by James I in 1617, to the Puritan mind condoned and encouraged activities which impeded disciplined progress towards holiness, for it detailed types of recreation, such as archery and dancing, which were permitted on Sunday. Precisely to counter the growing Puritan Sabbatarianism, the seemingly excessive strictness in refraining from all secular enjoyment on Sunday, Charles I in 1633 reissued the declaration calling for the Book of Sports to be read and followed. But Charles I added a fresh injunction: clergy who refused to publish the Book of Sports and read it from their pulpits would be deprived of their positions. All clergy of Puritan inclination or persuasion were thereby threatened with the loss of their jobs and possible civil recrimination if they followed their consciences and declined to heed the order. As a result of his noncompliance, Pastor Chauncy was ejected from his pulpit and chose to flee the country rather than face probable prosecution. The family arrived in Plymouth in May 1638, and the godly minister was soon settled at the church there. After a subsequent and somewhat controversial pastorate at Scituate, he was named the second president of fledgling Harvard College in 1654, serving until his death in 1672 as a tireless advocate of education and of a learned clergy.[2]

President Chauncy fathered seven sons—all Harvard graduates—and one daughter. The eldest son returned to England, settling first as a minister in Woodborough and then as a medical doctor in London. He named his oldest son Charles, and in turn, this Charles migrated to Boston where he pursued a career as a small merchant, distinguished only by his membership in the Ancient and Honorable Artillery Company of Boston. He did, however, marry into a family of some prominence. His wife, Sarah Walley, was the daughter of a Massachusetts Supreme Court judge and sister to the wife of the Reverend Joseph Sewall. The links between the Chauncys and the Sewalls were to remain intimate throughout the eighteenth century. The union of Charles and Sarah Chauncy produced four children. The eldest, a son christened Charles, was born January 1, 1705.[3]

We know little of the early life of Charles Chauncy. Whatever information to be gleaned from perusal of his private papers is lost, for Chauncy ordered them destroyed.[4] His father died in 1711, but his mother apparently remarried. The young Charles enrolled in the Boston public Latin School in 1712 to prepare for admission to Harvard College, where he finally matriculated June 14, 1717. Because his immediate family had meager resources, the means for financing his education remain a mystery. Chauncy's tuition bills at Harvard were paid in dry goods, but we do not know who supplied them. Presumably Chauncy entered into student life of the day with enthusiasm and zest, not always directing attention to academics, since before he received his B.A. in July 1721 he had been fined for card playing.[5]

The rigid discipline which was to characterize his later life had yet to manifest itself, but his scholarly potential did not go unnoticed. On June 11, 1722 Chauncy returned to Harvard, receiving first a fellowship from the John Walley bequest and then a subsidy of ten pounds per year from the Hollis endowment, before being named a "scholar of the House" for three years.[6] In October 1722 he became a charter member of the

Spy Club, a literary and debating group whose members read papers to each other and published a literary magazine, the first of its kind in an American college. His affiliation with a circle concerned with belles lettres is somewhat curious, given his expressed distaste for literature. As one of his peers noted, "He had so little idea of poetry, that he could never relish it, and wished that someone would translate Paradise Lost into prose that he might understand it."[7] He was perhaps more adept at logical argumentation, for when he received his M.A. in 1724, he was designated to represent the Masters at the commencement and chose to discourse on "Christ the Eternal Mediator."

But one could not remain cloistered at Harvard forever. Accordingly, after joining Old South Church in 1724, Chauncy began the expected routine of seeking a pastoral call. The groundwork had already been laid by the extended stay at Harvard spent reading theology and through occasional opportunities to preach in nearby pulpits, including that of his uncle, Joseph Sewall, at Old South. In the winter of 1724–1725 the would-be pastor became an active candidate for the vacant assistantship at Ipswich. His competition for the post was an old Harvard classmate, Nathaniel Rogers. After the congregation had ample opportunity to hear each preach and get to know them personally, the vote was taken. Chauncy received just one of the forty-five cast. Perhaps already the passionless argument, the virtually lifeless logical movement from point to point, which was to mark his later preaching and writing was manifesting itself, and a people eager to have both heart and head moved by the power of the spoken word chose his rival. As a later anecdote had it, "Once when [Chauncy] remarked that he besought God never to make him an orator, a kind friend replied that the prayer had been unequivocally granted."[8] Or as a twentieth century interpreter noted, "He never swept a congregation off its feet, either by oratorical eloquence or by persuading it of the very presence of the Spirit of God in its midst."[9] Early on, then, Chauncy gave evidence of what later became a total opposition both to enthusiasm in the pulpit and to a preaching style which relied on an appeal to the emotions.

In August 1725, Chauncy did receive a call to serve as assistant to William Waldron at Boston's New Brick Church. While he debated whether to accept, a more prestigious possibility presented itself. In 1725, the presidency of Harvard College became vacant, and the Board of Overseers named Benjamin Wadsworth of Boston's First Church to the post. Now the position of assistant to Thomas Foxcroft at New England's most influential congregation became available. Hence Chauncy declined the offer at New Brick to gamble on his chances to secure the best pastoral job open at the time. This effort was crowned with success, for when the congregation balloted, Chauncy received sixty-four votes, and his competitor, William Welsteed, garnered only forty-three. Welsteed in turn accepted the offer at New Brick which Chauncy had rejected.[10]

Chauncy began what was to become a nearly sixty year association with First Church in the fall of 1727. New England ecclesiastical practice decreed that only persons called to settle in particular covenanted congregations could be ordained. The first order of business at First Church after Chauncy accepted the call became planning a special service of ordination and installation for the new assistant. But ordinations were not simply affairs of individual congregations. Clergy from other churches would be invited to participate in or at least attend the service, and their presence not only symbolized the acceptance of the ordinand into the ranks of an increasingly professionalized clergy, but also served as a stamp of approval on the theological views of the man in question.[11] Among the Boston Congregational pastors of the day, none could claim to be a more vigorous standard-bearer of the old Puritan orthodoxy than Cotton Mather of the Second Church, and it was he who offered the right hand of fellowship when Chauncy was ordained October 25, 1727.[12]

In 1727, Boston was a lively place.[13] Long a center of colonial commercial and social life, the city was accustomed to dominating New England affairs. But in many respects, what made Boston exciting was a curious tension between the old and the new, for Boston was a city in transition. For years, the standard urban problems had challenged the city. The presence of prostitutes and the poor, saloons and restless sailors, troubled not only the ghosts of Boston's ancestors, but scores of preachers and devout Puritans who wondered whether decay was finally eroding the "city on a hill."

Over the next decade or so, the primacy of Boston would be threatened as commercial rivals emerged in Newport, New York, and Charleston. In addition, the back country, the settlements in the Connecticut River valley, began to press political, economic, and religious interests which defied the vested concerns of the Boston elite. On the religious scene, the pluralism which was to become a hallmark of American life taxed the hegemony of Boston's Puritan establishment. Anglicans, Quakers, Baptists—all once anathema to Puritan Boston—not only flourished but were gaining ever greater respectability. And for over a quarter century, the Congregationalists themselves had endured increasing internal dissent. The rise to prominence of the Brattle Street Church, founded in 1699 on a then extreme liberal revamping of Puritan principles, symbolized the heterodoxy which was replacing the old Puritan orthodoxy. Chauncy's Boston had long ceased to be the holy city envisioned in the dreams of its founders, but what Boston was becoming was not at all clear.

If the city stood with one foot in the past and the other in an uncertain future, First Church itself was a strange blend of the old and the new in New England religious life. Attended by many of the province's leading mercantile families, it stood at the head of the churches in the city, if not in the colony as a whole. Its relatively affluent membership, however, was more and more associated with that perceived decline in religious fervor and piety which troubled so many in the opening decades of the eighteenth century. It was as if those who reaped success in the material world had done so at the expense of a vital spiritual faith. Gone were the days when prosperity signalled divine approval and blessing. Now it betokened a lack of concern for things of the soul, and Old Brick, as First Church was popularly called, represented the presumed religious decay and preoccupation with this world believed rampant in Massachusetts Bay. In some areas, though, First Church was a bulwark of Puritan orthodoxy, while other churches seemed ready to compromise with the fluctuating and liberalizing demands of a more secularized constituency. First Church had long held to the principle of strict congregational independency and had opposed the adoption of the Cambridge Platform of 1648 which granted synods advisory power among the churches. When the Synod of 1662 approved what has become known as the Half-Way Covenant, First Church refused to adopt it, preferring to adhere to the more rigorous standards of baptism and membership qualifications in force at the time of its founding in 1630.

But during Chauncy's tenure, important changes occurred. The church voted to adopt the half-way measures March 31, 1731, and in 1736 began the practice of offering baptism to all adults, regardless of their parents' religious status. In 1731 the congregation also decided to discontinue the requirement of a personal testimony of religious experience on the part of candidates for membership, relying on the judgment of the pastors as to the state of a person's soul. In the aftermath of the Great Awakening when many again sought to protect churches from impurity by reinstituting a confession of faith as a prerequisite for admission into full membership, Old Brick held firm and in 1756 voted to continue its own practice.[14]

Important practical and intellectual consequences emerged from these changes. On a pragmatic level, the shifts no doubt made First Church more competitive with other congregations which drew from the same membership base. Some of the city's leading families had already aligned with the brazenly liberal Brattle Street Church, while others were drawn to the socially prestigious Anglican communion at King's Chapel. But the changes were not radical moves which drew Old Brick out of the Puritan mainstream. By the time of Chauncy's pastorate, the Half-Way Covenant and greater leniency with regard to the sacraments had already gained general respectability. To sanction some change had become "seasonable" if the Puritan way were to remain viable. And, ironically, many of the changes had gained their credibility first at Northampton in the Connecticut Valley, where Chauncy's first major antagonist, Jonathan Edwards, began his ministry the same year Chauncy came to First Church. On an intellectual level, the changes revealed the growing respect for the private, individualistic nature of religious experience and the belief that rational acceptance of Christian belief and nurture in the faith —both keystones of Chauncy's later opposition to the highly emotional, public conversion experience that he saw as characteristic of the evangelical approach—provide an orderly and valid route to divine grace.

But Chauncy was as concerned about his image as a pastor as he was about guiding orderly change at First Church. Indeed, New England had long regarded the clergy as exemplars of the holy life. As such, ministers were to be models not only of religious devotion, but also of the style of life expected of moral men. New England also still paid lip service to the institution of the family as the core component of the social order.[15] Hence a good marriage was incumbent upon him who would be both minister and model to the people of God. Shortly after his settlement at Old Brick, Chauncy began to make earnest plans for marriage. Again the links with the prominent Sewall family served him well. In the home of his uncle, Joseph Sewall, had lived for some ten years a young lady named Elizabeth Hirst, the daughter of Judge Grove Hirst and a granddaughter of Chief Justice Samuel Sewall. We do not know the details of the courtship; we may assume that since Chauncy had been a frequent guest at the Sewall home as nephew, member of the congregation, and occasional preacher at the Old South meetinghouse, he had sufficient opportunity to win the affections of Elizabeth Hirst. On May 9, 1728, Chauncy took this "most pretty, pleasant, virtuous, discreet, good Tempd Gentlewoman" as his wife.[16] As a family man, Chauncy would now require a higher salary and a parsonage. Accordingly, the congregation increased his compensation to four pounds ten shillings per week and set about to evict the tenants from a house the church owned to provide a decent home for the young assistant and his wife.[17] To the marriage of Charles and Elizabeth Chauncy were born three children: Charles (May 16, 1729), Elizabeth (November 21, 1731), and Sarah (September 22, 1732).[18]

As has been noted, Chauncy's early years as a Boston parson were rather quiet ones. But quietness did not mean inactivity. The post at First Church carried with it an automatic seat on the Harvard Board of Overseers. Chauncy attended his first meeting in the spring of 1728 and remained active in affairs of the College until the closing years of his life. In Boston itself, he quickly accepted those nonecclesiastical responsibilities which traditionally fell to the Puritan cleric. Shortly after his arrival at First Church, he joined with several of his fellow Boston clergymen in signing a protest calling for the prohibition of dueling after a man had been killed in a duel on Boston Common.[19] On March 11, 1728, Chauncy for the first time fulfilled one of the civic duties expected of the preacher by offering prayer at the opening of the town meeting.[20] His commitment to advancing educational causes led him in 1736 to offer public support to Joseph Kent, who had proposed opening a school in Boston which would specialize in mathematical study.[21]

The Puritan cleric, while presumably laboring among his convenanted people, also kept an eye on religious affairs outside the boundaries of his parish. And although protocol decreed that one minister did not interfere in the work of another, frequent interchanges occurred. The clergy of the province had been meeting annually for many years to discuss matters of mutual concern, usually bemoaning a perceived decline in evangelical piety. The widely known public lecture held each Thursday in Boston also served as an opportunity for clergy to confer with each other. At dinner after the lecture or in the home of one of the Boston preachers, pastors would gather to analyze the lectures and keep abreast of each other's activities. In addition, on those occasions when individual congregations experienced conflict with a pastor, other clergy and lay persons would form an advisory council to mediate, although their recommendations were not binding. Serving on such councils also offered the colony's pastors opportunities to become acquainted with each other, to appraise each other's strengths and weaknesses, and to determine who would be friend or foe if later controversies erupted.

In Boston, other opportunities for interchange occurred, for preachers often exchanged pulpits or invited peers to preach in their churches. This practice, besides reducing the number of sermons each had to prepare, both advanced a spirit of friendship among the clergy and promoted a facade of uniformity of belief. Then there were those special services long a part of the Massachusetts religious scene—days of prayer, days of thanksgiving, days of humiliation, and the like —when the clergy would combine talents for the spiritual edification of the entire citizenry.

From his position at Old Brick, Chauncy engaged from time to time in all these "at large" pastoral activities. For example, he frequently exchanged preaching services with Joseph Sewall and Thomas Prince at Old South Church, Samuel and William Cooper of the Brattle Street Church, and Samuel Checkley, pastor at New South; and in August 1734 he led a Day of Prayer service at Old South.[22] When Josiah Cotton undertook a mission assignment among the nine Congregationalist families living in Providence, Rhode Island, in 1731, Chauncy dutifully joined with 31 others to make a four year pledge to underwrite Cotton's support until such time as he had gathered a congregation sufficient to sustain its own expenses. The contribution signalled Chauncy's endorsement of a traditional form of evangelism, and the pledge itself served to authenticate Cotton's orthodoxy. In 1734 Cotton briefly returned to Boston to be married and sought out Chauncy to officiate at the ceremony.[23]

Chauncy was also called to serve on a council. The church at Eastham in 1740 proposed to dismiss its pastor, Samuel Osborn, on grounds of Arminianism; several clergy, including Chauncy, protested vigorously, and a subsequent investigation vindicated Osborn of the charge.[24] Chauncy did not issue a public statement of his own in the Osborn case, but merely added his name to those who signed the Council's report clearing Osborn. But if Chauncy's behavior at later councils might serve as an indication of his views in this case, one may be sure that he was less concerned with the theological fine points of Osborn's supposed Arminianism than he was with the potential danger to New England church order which might follow on Osborn's dismissal. If Osborn were dismissed, other congregations might presume that they, too, could challenge their pastors' orthodoxy. Such challenges in the end could not only destroy the traditional authority of pastors in guiding the religious life of their congregations and, indeed, of the colony, but could also undermine the entire religious order of New England, predicated as it was on congregations of believers directed by properly ordained ministers. As a rule, Chauncy throughout his life supported the clergy who observed the traditional decorum of the New England way.

In his own ministry, Chauncy was first and foremost a traditional Puritan cleric, devoting up to fifteen hours each day to the study of the Scriptures and theology. A family event helped focus his scholarly attention in the opening years of his career. In 1732, Addington Davenport, the husband of Chauncy's wife's sister and son of one of the founders of the

Brattle Street Church, committed what was to the orthodox Puritan mind the ultimate religious error: he left the Congregationalist household and entered the Church of England. After journeying to the mother country to obtain Anglican orders, the former lawyer returned to New England as a missionary at Scituate under the auspices of the Society for the Propagation of the Gospel. He then became lecturer at King's Chapel in Boston and later was named the first rector of Boston's Trinity Church.[25] With a defection so close to home, Chauncy began an intensive study of the nature of the episcopal office, perhaps to justify in his own mind the continuing validity of the New England Way. Davenport had become an Anglican, according to Chauncy, "upon this pretence, that it was a certain fact, that Episcopacy, in the appropriated sence [sic], was the form of government in the church from the time of the Apostles and down along through all successive ages."[26]

Chauncy set out to prove that such was not the case. By the spring of 1734 he had finished a manuscript detailing the results of his investigation, and on May 30 advertised in the Boston *News-Letter* for subscribers to its publication. While his efforts failed and the manuscript remained unpublished for nearly forty years, his stance was apparently well known. Anglican convert Timothy Cutler, in a letter dated November 8, 1734, offered a harsh appraisal: "The proposals are from Charles Chauncy, a Teacher of this Town, who has but a little time ago begun his Enquiries, and not above a month ago before the Publication of his Proposals profess'd himself to a Churchman as an Enquirer then. . . . I suppose no thinking Person will be shock't by the daughty Performance of this Insidious Person."[27] But if Chauncy's manuscript found no takers, his interest in episcopal polity did not die. It merely lay dormant until the 1760s when a Church of England plan to establish an American bishopric made such concerns the religious topic of the day.

But Chauncy was beginning to become a public figure. During his first decade at Old Brick, four of his funeral discourses appeared in print as did his 1734 Artillery Company election sermon. On the whole, the published sermons followed the standard Puritan structure: Scripture text, statement of the doctrine derived from the text, explication of its meaning, and the application of the doctrine or "uses" in everyday life. The sermon delivered at the annual election of officers of the Boston Artillery Company belongs in the class of sermons regularly preached at public occasions. Every year the Artillery Company invited one of the Boston pastors to preach when officers were named, just as every year the colony's General Court honored one of the Bay clergy by requesting that he preach at the opening legislative session. Hearkening back to an earlier era in Puritan Massachusetts when the ideals of theocracy prevailed, these sermons offered ministers an opportunity to address public issues. In time, the election sermons especially became a forum for promulgating Puritan political philosophy and serve as a barometer of political opinion among the colony's leadership. As a matter of routine, the election and Artillery Company sermons were published. In the funeral sermons, Chauncy also echoed many traditional themes of Puritan preaching: the frailty of life, the ways in which religion shapes character, the need for sincerity in religion. Yet he also fashioned emphases which would become characteristics of his opposition to the evangelical thrust of the 1740s and his approach to any controversy.

Chauncy's sermon on June 3, 1734, when the Artillery Company members elected officers, contains little which would distinguish it from other sermons of its type.[28] But it does indicate a pride in local military potential, a pride which would move to the mainstream of Chauncy's thinking by the time of the later French and Indian Wars. When Chauncy spoke in 1734, New England had witnessed two decades of relative peace. Queen Anne's War, as the War of the Spanish Succession became known in America, had concluded in 1713. During the war, Massachusetts saw more action than the other English colonies, with the settlement at Deerfield suffering virtually total destruction. But the years of peace brought a decline of enthusiasm for matters of a military sort; interest in militia training had waned. Hence Chauncy was particularly pleased to applaud a revival of martial spirit in the Boston Artillery Company because he believed that it was always necessary for a people to guard their own safety. More importantly, he claimed that those who were colonial military leaders deserved proper recognition for their loyalty. Before many years would pass he would echo that theme, when British policy required all colonial officers to serve in subordinate capacities to British officers, even if of the same rank. Then as now, Chauncy took pride in the abilities of the volunteers who comprised the Artillery Company, convinced that their military skill was on a par with the best Britain had to offer.

In two of the funeral sermons, one preached at the service for Sarah Byefield, wife of Province Council member and Vice-Admiralty Judge Nathanael Byefield, and one for seventeen-year-old Elizabeth Price, Chauncy called upon his listeners to make diligent use of the "means of grace" in preparing for death as well as in nurturing the religious life.[29] Use of the "means of grace" was a hallmark of Puritan piety. The means were aids given by God through the ministry of the Church to foster individual spiritual growth and development. The three which Chauncy particularly recommended were meditation (especially on one's impending death), regular reading of the Bible, and frequent attendance on the preaching of the Word. The means offered a structure and framework for the religious life. And Chauncy was to be propelled by a passion for order and a fear of disorder until his own death.

In another of the funeral sermons, Chauncy argued that true religion consisted of an inward feeling or motive.[30] It was not to be found in outward appearances only. Religion which consisted mainly of public demonstrations of piety was little more than show. The same idea would recur frequently in Chauncy's attacks on the emotional excesses of the Great Awakening.

The fourth in its style and content reflected the form of the Puritan jeremiad.[31] Essentially a lament for a mythical past when New Englanders were presumably more religious, the jeremiad was a call to return to a more devout religious style. In the sermon, Chauncy noted that many prominent churchmen had died recently. He concluded that deaths of the truly faithful came as a sign from God to mark the degeneracy of the times. The lesson was not simply to recognize that true piety had disappeared, but also to turn to prayer in order to mold one's life after the model of those who were now dead. But this discourse likewise gave its audience a glimpse of Chauncy's personality, for its title, "Prayer for Help a Seasonable Duty," betrayed Chauncy's penchant for emphasizing what was appropriate to the circumstances. "Seasonable" in a technical sense denotes a line of thinking or a course of action which is particularly appropriate to a given situation. When good men died, it was "seasonable" to pray. In time, when revivals upset the religious order of New England, it would be "seasonable" to issue a summons for a less emotional approach to religious experience. In time, too, it would be "seasonable" to protest the possible appointment of an Anglican bishop for the colonies. Later it would be "seasonable" to support the movement for American independence from Britain, and ultimately it would be "seasonable" to rethink the contours of Puritan theology in order to preserve the New England way. Indeed, it would always, for Chauncy, be "seasonable" to preserve the fabric of New England structures and traditions.

But for the moment, events served to focus Chauncy's concern on his pastoral work at First Church. In 1736 his senior associate, Thomas Foxcroft, suffered a severe stroke, leaving him partially paralyzed for the remainder of his life. Although Chauncy technically remained Foxcroft's assistant until after the latter's death in 1769, he now had more of the pastoral responsibilities of First Church thrust into his hands. The increased investment of time in parish affairs meant less time for study and sustained scholarly inquiry. Foxcroft was able to resume some of his duties in time, but Chauncy remained essentially at the helm from 1736 until the congregation voted to hire him an associate in 1778.

Within the family circle changes likewise occurred. In the spring of 1737 Chauncy's wife became seriously ill. She died May 13 that year and was buried three days later, leaving the ambitious minister with three young children to raise. But Chauncy could little add the responsibility of being a single parent to his other obligations nor long endure life without the companionship of a wife. Puritan tradition readily sanctioned remarriage, so Chauncy's search for a second wife was far from unusual. He found a second bride in an attractive young widow named Elizabeth Phillips Townshend, "a Gentlewoman of very plentiful Estate."[32] Indeed, there is little doubt that the new Mrs. Chauncy came from a more sophisticated background than her husband and brought both higher financial standing and enhanced social prestige to the increasingly prominent assistant at Old Brick. After their marriage on January 8, 1739, Elizabeth Chauncy moved into the parsonage with her daughter, Rebecca, and immediately undertook renovating the home.[33] She was to remain mistress of the busy household until her death in 1757.

The quiet years at the beginning of a career were about to end for Charles Chauncy. George Whitefield arrived in New England in 1740, preaching at Boston in Chauncy's pulpit at First Church. The Great Awakening had begun, and Chauncy was not at all pleased with its progress.

2.

Preserving the Puritan Way

George Whitefield, an early associate of John Wesley in the evangelical movement in England, arrived in the American colonies in 1739. After a brief stay in Georgia, he embarked on a journey which would carry him through most of the major settlements in British North America. Ostensibly his goal was to raise funds for an orphanage which he had helped establish in Georgia. But Whitefield was too much the preacher to let an occasion pass without seeking to win converts to the Christian cause. Accordingly, his wandering labors became a travelling revival, a "great and general awakening" to the religious sensibilities which folk romantically associated with the faith of their forebears, a reveille to a piety centered in an affective religious experience. When he entered New England, he found that numerous forces had prepared the way for his call to salvation. Not all these forces were religious, but all did at least contribute to a broadly based sense of unsettledness among his listeners.

Determining causes of a major event like the Great Awakening puts any historian on dangerous ground, for rarely does a single or simple explanation provide a satisfying and sufficiently comprehensive interpretation of what remains complex and elusive. Economics, politics, the psychology of social identity—all serve as clues in unravelling what remains first and foremost a religious event. And many tensions operated in the religious sector itself in the age of the Awakening, feeding into the total matrix of energies which blossomed into the revival. Perhaps foremost among the religious tensions was that between emotion and reason, at best always in delicate balance in mainstream Christian thought, but particularly so in Puritan ideology. Edwin S. Gaustad, in his classic treatment of the Awakening in New England, capsuled the many nuances of this tension in the juxtaposition of Pietism and the Enlightenment.[1] In the revivals, proponents felt that the restraints of reason (the worst of what was symbolized by "Enlightenment") had degenerated into a tyranny against the free expression of religious feeling, while opponents believed an unshackled emotionalism (the worst of what was symbolized by "Pietism") could bring religious anarchy. Neither wished one exclusively without the other, but none was satisfied with the uneasy balance which was about to crack by 1740 when George Whitefield's tour of the colonies brought him to New England.

Another sign of danger in the Puritan religious order had been present overtly for fifty years and covertly for decades more. In 1691, the new charter officially transforming Massachusetts Bay into a royal colony required minimal toleration of Christian religious groups which did not adhere to Puritan views. By Chauncy's day, Anglican, Baptist, and Quaker places of worship flourished in Boston, attracting some of the colony's leading families. Resented at first and reluctantly tolerated at best, these groups were visible signs that routes to divine grace other than those sanctioned by Puritan thinking were not only plausible, but attractive. In the seventeenth century, it had been possible to ban Quakers and banish the likes of Roger Williams, who had undercut the Puritan concept of religious order with his unique ideas of freedom of conscience.[2] But when Chauncy ministered at First Church, he had to accept the presence of a multiplicity of religious options within the former stronghold of New England Puritanism.

In the social sector, New England was in the throes of a

controversy with serious economic and political implications. In 1740, Massachusetts stood on the brink of economic depression because it lacked an adequate circulating currency. A group headed by John Colman renewed an earlier proposal for the establishment of a "bank" in which unsold land would become the basis for a paper money currency.[3] Many advocates of the scheme were proprietors in newly chartered towns and prospering middle-class businessmen. In addition, the land bank proposal drew support from several Boston merchants and businessmen, including Samuel Adams, brewer and father of the patriot. The opposition to the bank, however, came almost exclusively from the most wealthy Boston merchants and the circle closest to Governor Jonathan Belcher. They countered with a plan to establish a silver bank. To its advocates, the land bank had a clear economic advantage. With the value of unsold land as a new standard and guarantee for currency, more paper money could be printed. With more money in circulation, those who wielded little economic power would more easily be able to secure loans, repay outstanding debts, and improve their financial situation. To its opponents, the bank seemed destined to end their place of economic privilege in the social order, for it would allow greater numbers of people to be financially independent of them.

Implementation of the proposal involved an excursion in politics, for control of the provincial government, which would charter such a bank, lay in the hands of the opposition. If land bankers could be elected in large numbers to the General Court, power would pass from aristocratic Boston to the smaller, less commercially oriented towns. Many new towns had been established away from the coastal area in the preceding decades, but few had bothered to elect representatives to the legislative assembly with any regularity. In other words, representation did not reflect changes in population growth and land ownership patterns. In addition, there were strong links between the power elite and the Crown. When the English monarchy was regaining power and more aggressively asserting royal prerogatives in colonial affairs in the latter part of the seventeenth century, Massachusetts had been granted its new charter. The 1691 charter, in making the Bay Colony a royal colony, now required that the governor be appointed by the British government rather than elected by the people. But over the years, these crown-appointed governors and the Boston elite who dominated the Assembly and the Council had developed a rather close working relationship which posed little threat to operative authority patterns. When the economic crisis reflected in the coin shortage came to a head, the towns and bank advocates recognized that the colonial legislature was the only organized body which could deal with the situation effectively, but knew that opponents controlled it. If the towns began to elect a full complement of delegates—two each—to the Assembly, they would gain control of the legislature and would then be able to use it as a vehicle to authorize the creation of a land bank. Once the Boston elite lost control of Assembly and Council, the working coalition with crown officials would topple and the political landscape of the colony would take on a new cast.

The strength of the land bankers peaked in May 1741 when, despite the fact that Governor Belcher had recently jailed their leaders, proponents garnered a majority in the lower house in the annual election. The "Patriot party," as the land bankers were called, barely had time to flex its muscles when Parliament intervened and prohibited the establishment of a colonial land bank under terms of the 1721 "Bubble Act." Between sessions of the Assembly, however, the bank had started operation extralegally. It fell to Governor William Shirley, Belcher's more popular successor, to superintend its dissolution. Nevertheless, the energies released by the controversy did not wane when the land bank ceased to be a viable remedy to cure Massachusetts' financial ills, but surfaced again in the Awakening.

In addition, the Awakening was far from being simply a

New England movement. Indeed, the general character of the revivals and the rapidity with which they spread throughout the colonies mark the Awakening, in the eyes of some analysts, as the first expression of a distinctively American identity in the English areas of North America.[4] While the colonies were technically separate individual entities, each with its own charter determining its relation to the mother country, they had more and more in common. The Awakening, because it ultimately affected all the colonies, gave them not only their first shared "crisis," in the widespread disruption of prevailing religious patterns, but also the first stages of a common sense of destiny and a commitment to the belief that God had appointed the American people as special agents in carrying history to its consummation.[5] The challenge to the authority of established religious ways—whether the authority of the clergy over religious life or the hegemony of particular churches over given regions—which came with the Awakening easily fused with the challenge to the authority of king and Parliament over colonial politics, latent in the gnawing discontent with British imperial policy over the land bank and other issues, to generate one constellation of influences which helped precipitate the later movement for independence. And, as Richard Bushman and William G. McLoughlin have suggested, a host of other factors—from the problems of coping with an expanding population, the sense of an impending shortage of land, and a conviction that real local power in the colonies still remained in the hands of the few—lurked in the background.[6]

In New England, clearly, the dominance of established Puritan order in matters civil and religious and the viability of Puritanism as a religious style were thus in danger. If alternatives succeeded, the Puritan tradition would collapse. Puritanism could receive new life through a reshaping of its perspective, which kept essential features while updating its defenses, or through a revival of dedication and commitment to the old ways. The zealous and contagious enthusiasm of George

Whitefield seemed to make the latter choice more attractive. But even before Whitefield arrived in New England, religious stirrings were in process. In the mid-1730s the young pastor at Northampton, Jonathan Edwards, had guided his flock through a brief period of intensified interest in religion reminiscent of the "harvests" which had five times swept the parish in the Connecticut Valley under the leadership of his grandfather and predecessor, the illustrious Solomon Stoddard. But by the closing years of the decade, the fire had become a heap of ashes. Whitefield stoked it back to life. The response to his dynamism was overwhelming. Witness the following newspaper capsule of his days in Boston:

> Last Thursday Evening the Rev'd Mr. Whitefield arrived from Rhode-Island, being met on the Road and conducted to Town by several Gentlemen. The next Day in the Forenoon he attended Prayers in the King's Chappel, and in the Afternoon he preach'd to a vast Congregation in the Rev'd Dr. Colman's Meeting-House. The next Day he preach'd in the Forenoon at the South Church to a Crowded Audience, and in the Afternoon to about 5000 People on the Common: and Lord's Day in the afternoon having preach'd to a great Number of People at the Old Brick Church, the House not being large enough to hold those that crowded to hear him, when the Exercise was over, He went and preached in the Field, to at least 8000 Persons.[7]

After approximately six weeks, Whitefield left New England, but the religious revival continued, pushed to a higher pitch by the subsequent arrival of two other wandering preachers, Gilbert Tennant, who had already had several revivalistic sermons published in Boston, and James Davenport, who made numerous excursions into New England between 1741 and 1743. But while the people came in droves to sit at the feet of these itinerants and have their hearts stirred and their religious sensibilities heightened, Charles Chauncy remained aloof, growing increasingly upset at the trend. At first he thought that he alone of the Boston clergy had qualms about the value of the revival.

Chauncy's complaints had both theological and institutional bases. On the theological side, he was upset by the revivalists' stress on an emotionally charged experience of conversion as the starting point of the religious life and their emphasis on the doctrine of assurance. Institutionally the practice of itinerancy appeared to Chauncy to strike the death blow to the time-honored structure of a clergy settled among a convenanted people. To express his rage, he took to the pulpit, preaching numerous diatribes against presumed evangelical errors. He turned to the press, publishing numerous sermons and tracts against the Awakening. And he worked behind the scenes, travelling several hundred miles through the Bay Colony to gather documentation for his claims, meeting with other ministers who had reservations about the revivals, and orchestrating a gradual crescendo of opposition to the movement. Along the way, of course, he encountered numerous foes, individuals who saw the Awakening as the harbinger of a new day in New England's religious history.

Chauncy's primary adversary in dispute over the merits of the revivals was not the illustrious Whitefield, the vitriolic Tennant, or the notorious Davenport. As itinerants, Whitefield, Tennant, and Davenport were transitional characters—they came and left or were asked to leave. Instead, Chauncy confronted the dignified Jonathan Edwards, the most articulate and probably the most judicious defender of the evangelical surge, in a sustained paper war.[8] Much of later history has viewed Chauncy solely from the perspective that he and Edwards squared off as ideological and theological sparring partners without carefully examining what Chauncy himself had to say. Captive to Edwards's theological genius and critical insight, commentators have tended to label Chauncy simply as a half-hearted and hardly imaginative liberal, a forerunner of later Unitarianism, or a Deist in Puritan disguise.[9] Most have named Edwards winner of the contest because when Edwards, the fomenter of the Awakening, became Edwards, the critic of the Awakening, he condemned many of the same revival phenomena which had horrified Chauncy. But Chauncy and Edwards were fiercely loyal to the Puritan tradition as they received it, and in the writings from this era both quoted the same "orthodox" Puritan divines to bolster apparently contradictory positions. Each simply took the main tenets and spirit of New England Puritanism and pushed them to very logical but very different extremes.

Perry Miller has wisely suggested that in their confrontation Edwards's watchword was "sensible," but Chauncy's remained "seasonable."[10] Chauncy absorbed that strand in the Puritan heritage which observed that God usually worked in orderly ways to prepare the individual for the presence of the Spirit. Edwards, however, responded to the strain which saw salvation essentially as an affective apprehension of the beauty and excellency of God which involved the whole person. This understanding might come at times, in places, and in visible ways humans could not blueprint in advance. For Edwards, salvation was the supernatural sense experience *par excellence* which one lived moment by moment in spiritual ecstasy. Accordingly, he centered true religion in the affections, but without discarding the role of the rational element in human nature. Edwards referred to the religious affections as "affections of the mind," and one of his interpreters suggested that for Edwards, religion always denoted a particular kind of ethical and emotional response to "a specific intellectual stimulation."[11]

He did not believe that the rational process in the individual after conversion was distinct from that process before conversion, but he did posit a qualitative intuitional difference which meant that only spiritual persons could grasp the reality of God which caused and yet transcended rational structures. Accordingly, Edwards spoke of religious experience as instilling a "new principle of life" in the individual, one in which the spiritual sense brought such a unity of inclination, will, mind, and heart that the terms became synonymous.[12] For him, the inclination-will-mind-heart matrix could be distinguished from the understanding (the power of perception, speculation, discernment, and judgment), and religious experience belonged to the former. In contrast, Chauncy believed that the understanding was the locus of religious experience and therefore regarded the evangelical approach as a delusion which lured the unthinking into false religion. So little use did he have for Edwards's subtle construction of religious experience that some twenty-five years after the Awakening had ebbed, he still labelled Edwards "a visionary enthusiast, and not to be minded in anything he says."[13]

Chauncy asserted the primacy of reason in religious experience because he viewed the rational process as integrating individual experiences of all sorts into a unified whole in much the same way as covenant structures brought coherence to common life. Conversion, while orienting the direction of the individual towards godliness, brought no radical disjuncture with past experience. It transpired in the context of the continuous orderly work of a gracious God in drawing His creatures to Himself.[14] Indeed, God had appointed "means of grace" —attendance on the sacraments, the preaching of the Word, the ministrations of the clergy, private reading of the Scripture —designed to bring human beings logically and rationally to an acceptance of the gift of salvation. Chauncy blasted the evangelicals because he believed that the emotionalism they aroused rendered this rational religious experience impossible: "But in nothing does the *enthusiasm* of these persons discover itself more, than in the disregard they express to the Dictates of *reason.* They are above the force of argument, beyond conviction from a calm and sober address to their understandings."[15]

In his major antirevival work, he raged because "good men" had been made "subjects of terror," doubting the authenticity of their experience of salvation if they had not manifested "bodily effects" at the time of conversion. Why, he pondered, should they be coerced to question their salvation simply because they confidently assumed rational understanding and acceptance of religious teaching and practice would lead to eternal bliss?[16] For Chauncy, salvation could reasonably be expected to come in due season to one who used the traditional "means of grace" and lived a moral life.

On the eve of the Awakening, Chauncy had published a sermon dealing specifically with the use of one of the appointed means of grace, the Lord's Supper. Arguing that rational moral persuasion was the only "force" proper to religion, Chauncy declared that even a sense of personal inadequacy and sinfulness ought not prevent one from participating in that sacrament, one of the most important means because its celebration had been commanded by Christ himself. Christ surely would not have commended the sacrament to sincere followers if he did not expect them to use it as a way to promote spiritual nurture.[17] In certain ages in times past, Chauncy noted, the church had even resorted to physical force to compel religious practice. Such abandonment of rational persuasion was as deplorable as that of evangelicals who substituted a complex emotional-psychological pressure for reasoned argument. He saw one ray of hope. " 'Tis worthy of our thankful Notice," he remarked, "that the Principles of *Liberty* are every Day gaining Ground in our *Nation.*"[18] In later years, "Principles of *Liberty*" of a different sort would be foremost in Chauncy's mind, but for the moment he was concerned primarily with a liberty which included at least the freedom to employ the tested means of the faith in anticipation of salvation and the freedom to abstain from other approaches.

Shortly after the revivals became widespread, Chauncy delivered Boston's Thursday lecture, speaking on the changes conversion brought to human life. In language occasionally reminiscent of Edwards, he outlined the marks of conversion for those uncertain about the state of their souls. Conversion occurred differently for different people, he asserted. Some might not even remember a discrete experience of conversion, for they may have been saved since childhood. In addition, as far as Chauncy was concerned, the type of conversion experience one had also depended on the nature and degree of sin which controlled one's preconversion life. Another variable centered on the multifaceted psychological composition of human beings. Certain gospel doctrines moved the "natural tempers" of some sinners, but not of others. Accordingly, Chauncy logically assumed that God used as many different forms of conversion as there were people. Hence if one believed one had been saved and now led a moral life marked by continuing reliance on the established "means of grace," one should not succumb to doubts triggered by the evangelical approach.[19]

In both these writings Chauncy emphasized the individualistic character of the salvific experience. In the revivals, despite Edwards's concern over excesses of emotion and enthusiasm, conversion experiences quickly became stereotyped. Bodily effects, those seemingly uncontrollable physical reactions to the supposed work of the Spirit, came to be a necessary ingredient of genuine conversion. Chauncy rebelled at this scheme and defended the liberty of the individual to pursue salvation according to the means available to all and the liberty for each to have a type of conversion "seasonable" to individual background and temperament. But a strong case may also be made for regarding individualism as a central thrust of the evangelical movement which Chauncy was attempting to counter. Although the evangelicals theoretically acknowledged the value of attendance on the "means of grace," they shifted the stress from patient waiting for the Spirit to work through the means to the necessity of an immediate all-consuming apprehension of the divine presence. Because the individual sinner became the center of religious experience and because all persons as sinners held equal status before God, the importance of the individual in the structure of both religion and society was enhanced. Social distinctions faded into the background since the single significant differential was whether the individual had directly experienced salvation.

To appreciate both positions, one must recall the intent of the covenant idea which had long been a controlling element in New England religion. The covenant structure provided a way for distinguishing between the regenerate and unregenerate within society, since those who had undergone a conversion experience could present themselves before the congregation to own the covenant, to bind themselves formally to the church and its teachings as members of the elect. Those who owned the covenant assumed a peculiar position in both the religious and political spheres in the early days of New England, since admission to both the sacraments and the franchise was available only to those who had entered the covenant relationship.

The Half-Way Covenant of 1662 eased the first restriction, and the 1691 charter modified franchise requirements. But the practical intention of the covenant remained clear: it was designed to leave control of both church and state in the hands of the converted through a hierarchical structure which made religious experience the criterion for social differentiation. One could move into the upper stratum only if one could testify to the work of the Spirit in effecting salvation. The Awakening, while recapturing the vitality of primal Puritan religious experience, nevertheless levelled a sharp blow to the remnants of the somewhat artificial covenant distinctions by regarding all persons as fundamentally equal because all were sinners.

The criterion for differentiation in society became an experience of assured conversion without its earlier sequel, submission to traditional authority encapsuled in covenant institutions. Evangelical individualism was an individualism outside formal structures and consequently left the established hierarchical model in ruins. Chauncy's brand of individualism likewise struck at the heart of the covenant system, but from a different vantage point. If the evangelicals had effectively destroyed the function of the covenant by replacing it with the conversion experience alone, Chauncy rendered the covenant valueless by his staunch insistence on the use of the "means of grace" as the only legitimate path to conversion. One exalted the individual because the Spirit could radically alter one's status; the other, because the individual had power to determine whether to take advantage of the pattern of life and conduct set forth in faithful adherence to the means. In other words, for Edwards and the evangelicals, the miracle was that election could come even to the individual no matter how worthy or unworthy in God's eyes, no matter how high or low in the eyes of the world.

For Chauncy, the miracle remained that God gave each individual the rational ability to comprehend religious truth presented by the divinely instituted church and then to follow the way to salvation. Each, then, contributed to a fuller appreciation of the individual, the evangelicals by making human experience the sole criterion of personal significance and Chauncy and his supporters by defending the freedom of the individual to act according to accepted procedures.

Chauncy argued his case further in a December 1741 Thursday lecture on the diversity of talents among the clergy. Chauncy always attached a positive value to such diversity, for he saw greater divine glory reflected in variety than in monotony and he believed that God worked in many ways to provide for the religious needs of differing sorts of people.[20] Within the ranks of the clergy Chauncy found men whose personalities and capabilities were designed to aid the work of the Spirit in differing ways. Not surprisingly, given his own predilection, the first "gift of the Spirit" to ministers which Chauncy sketched was the ability to reach the human understanding through rational persuasion.[21] But second place went to the power to move human passions, the heart of the evangelical approach as Chauncy observed it. Chauncy's point, however, was not to endorse the evangelical position, but to place the ability to arouse emotions subordinate to the skill of reaching the mind. "For the *human passions* are capable of serving valuable purposes in religion," he declared, "and may to good advantage be excited and warmed; always provided they are kept under the restraints of *reason;* for otherwise they will soon run wild, and may make those in whom they reign to do so too."[22] Chauncy could not totally deny the affective dimension of religious experience which the evangelicals exalted. But he affirmed the affective only if it remained under the control of the rational.

Concomitant with the evangelical stress on the affective in the experience of conversion came a fresh emphasis on the doctrine of assurance. If one believed that he or she had been brought by the Spirit into a saving relationship with God, how could one be sure the experience was genuine and not a Satan-inspired deception? If God had already determined who was elect, did it make any difference whether humans prepared themselves for salvation? Neither proponents nor opponents of the revivals wished to give to a mere human any role in gaining salvation which would deny the totally gratuitous nature of election. Such a move would smack of dreaded Arminianism and destroy the absolute sovereignty of God over affairs of the soul. But the psychological nature of the human creature meant that many were ill-content to devote their lives to the business of religion without some assurance of results. For those imbued with the evangelical spirit, the cataclysmic conversion experience provided its own authentication and assurance. Persons were visibly seized by a power not of their own making, and since the experience transpired within the context of religion, it was assumed to be of divine origin.

But what was the status of those who had no overwhelming religious experience with its internal verification? Were they outside the fold of the elect because they lacked the same assurance? Those who exhorted their followers to make diligent use of the "means of grace" without anticipation of a radical experience of conversion were clearly put on the defensive by the evangelicals who received assurance of election in the experience of conversion itself. But if the stress on the "means of grace" were abandoned in favor of independence on the immediate work of the Spirit, would not all order in religion disappear and the Puritan Way collapse?

Chauncy had briefly addressed the matter of assurance in *The New Creature Describ'd and Consider'd* (1741). It followed from his belief that the conversion experience could take many forms and that assurance was likewise multidimensional and geared to the needs of the individual. Accordingly, he denied that assurance came in an identical way to each who was saved, if it came at all. God simply gave each person the assurance one needed through faithful attendance on the "means of grace."[23] Chauncy continued his defense of dependence on the "means of grace" as the most viable route to salvation and assurance in a 1742 sermon on the doctrine of the Holy Spirit. On the surface one could hardly ask for a more orthodox statement of Puritan pneumatology, but Chauncy ably twisted Puritan doctrine to make his point. The Spirit came to humans not in visions, revelations, or trances induced by exhorters—all of which he associated with the evangelical stance—but through regular use of the appointed "means of grace." By faithfully attending to the appointed means, New England could not only await, but expect a genuine outpouring of the Holy Spirit, one more orderly than the enthusiastic excesses revivalists identified with the work of God.[24]

In his primary anti-evangelical tome, *Seasonable Thoughts on the State of Religion in New-England* (1743), Chauncy classified the evangelical stress on the immediate work of the Spirit and the belief that assurance was essential to genuine conversion as belonging to the "spirit of error" rampant at that time. He suggested that both led to antinomianism of the worst sort, since they abandoned all orderly guides for the conduct of spiritual life within which the individual grew in grace. It was time, he declared, to return to the ministrations of the settled clergy within the covenant structure as they shepherded men and women in the use of those means through which generations of New Englanders had ordered the approach to God.[25]

It was the threat to religious order generated by the practice of itineracy which finally drew other ministers to Chauncy's side. Since the standing order had allowed for clergy to preach occasionally in churches other than their own, when the Awakening mushroomed, pastors adept at provoking revivals were frequently invited to neighboring parishes to arouse the people there. But the most influential promoters of the revivals were the itinerants such as Whitefield, Tennant, and Davenport who simply went from place to place preaching and exhorting, with or without an invitation from the settled ministers to do so. In the last analysis the New England Way was unprepared for a situation in which men wandered about preaching wherever and whenever they could obtain a hearing, for it decreed that each ordained pastor had his own parish and refrained from interfering with the work of another ordained pastor in his parish. Itineracy not only violated the congregational principles of the self-sufficiency and absolute independence of each church and its pastor, but in the last analysis it was just ill-disguised interference in the ordered ministry of the settled clergy.

Whitefield was holding forth in Boston in May 1742 when the Congregational clergy of Massachusetts gathered for their annual convention. Although the majority of the ministers still endorsed the revivals, some who were beginning to entertain doubts about their value, those who would later be dubbed "Old Lights," met twice at Chauncy's home while the convention was in progress.[26] In addition to congratulating Chauncy on having recently received an honorary Doctor of Divinity degree from the University of Edinburgh, they discussed the state of religion in New England, focusing especially on the issue of assurance and the practice of itineracy. Some were even suspicious of Whitefield's integrity. If he was, as he claimed, travelling on behalf of his Georgia orphanage, why was he so eager to upset the standing order and what was he doing with the money he collected? "Chauncy, though incapable of appreciating such a man as Whitefield, was too good a judge of character to suspect him of intentional dishonesty."[27]

Later that summer the dangers inherent in itineracy became more pronounced when James Davenport, already *persona non grata* in Connecticut, marched to Massachusetts Bay. Davenport had alienated the standing order in Connecticut when he boldly declared that many of the regular clergy were not really Christians, that the people had a right to a Christian pastor, and that persons should not feel bound by the established covenant polity if they had a non-Christian pastor, but should remove him from his pulpit or secede from the parish and form a new one.[28] Consequently, when Davenport arrived in Boston, he found many of the clergy reluctant to permit him to preach in their meetinghouses. A small group, including the Anglican priest from Marblehead, gathered at Chauncy's home on July 8 to discuss Davenport's attacks on the clergy before going to hear him preach. At that stage, Davenport was dismissed as a mere rabble-rouser. As Ebenezer Parkman noted in his diary entry concerning the caucus at Chauncy's, ". . . few among the wise and worthy, but judge he [Davenport] is touched in the head."[29] The situation became more critical the next month when Davenport brazenly claimed that the Boston clergy were unconverted and singled out by name Benjamin Colman, Joseph Sewall, and Chauncy as the most conspicuous examples.[30] Davenport even visited Dr. Chauncy to inquire the "reason of hope" in him. Chauncy simply replied that Davenport had no business being in Boston, but belonged with his own congregation.[31]

Chauncy's published critiques of the Awakening all contained scathing attacks on itineracy. In an open letter to George Wishart in Scotland, he identified itineracy and emotionalism as the two primary problems facing New England religious life, declaring that these two phenomena had left the state of religion in worse shape than it had been before the revivals erupted. He closed the letter with a sharp attack on Davenport, blaming him directly for the disruption of religious order in New England.[32] Chauncy opened another hostile tract, *Enthusiasm Describ'd and Caution'd Against,* with a prefatory notice addressed to Davenport. After excoriating the itinerant for condemning Boston's settled pastors, he went on to say that he simply could not understand why Davenport had usurped the divine prerogative of judging the state of individual souls.[33] Interwoven with this assault was an attack on all who, under the presumed influence of the Spirit, left their appointed stations in life to take up others. It was a stinging indictment of itinerants and exhorters who left parishes or refused to be settled in parishes, presumably their appointed stations, to disrupt the orderly work of those who remained with their established vocations within the structure of the settled ministry.[34] As did many in the eighteenth century, Chauncy accepted a hierarchical model for society: each person had a given place and should remain in it.

When *Seasonable Thoughts* appeared as a counter to Jonathan Edwards's judicious defense of the Awakening, entitled *Some Thoughts on the State of Religion in New-England,* it provoked unrest among Awakening advocates on both sides of the Atlantic who thought it would severely impede their efforts.[35] Although the revivals had already begun to ebb when the book became available in 1743, Chauncy continued his blistering attack on itineracy, naming it the first "irregularity and disorder" connected with the "late *religious Appearances* in New England." He believed that itineracy not only implied that the settled clergy were unqualified for their positions, but that it threatened the dissolution of all church order as well. If all clergy became itinerant and none remained settled, the standing order and any semblance of religious authority would crumble.

Chauncy castigated itinerants for obstructing the liberty of the established clergy to carry on their work through criticisms and questions about their Christian character.[36] He went on to link itinerants with the enthusiastic aspects of the revivals when he noted that violent emotional and physical responses to conversion tended to transpire under their preaching more than under the watchful ministry of the standing order.[37] Indeed, itinerants whose slurs impeded the effective functioning of the settled clergy were the same ones who caused the people to doubt the validity of the divinely appointed "means of grace" and who substituted an antinomian enthusiasm in their place.

The divisions in the ranks of the clergy over the value of the revivals came to a head in late 1742 and 1743. At Boston's Second Church, for example, the congregation sought to dismiss one of its pastors, Samuel Mather, for holding supposedly liberal theological views. In actuality, Mather had become an ally of Chauncy in opposing the Awakening and was unpopular with his flock because they supported the revivals. An ecclesiastical council was summoned to advise the congregation, and Chauncy was invited to be a member. Chauncy recognized that the real issue was Mather's critical attitude towards the evangelical movement and therefore refused to sign the recommendation of dismissal presented to the council.[38] Chauncy may have been a minority, but the episode revealed the extent to which the Awakening had divided the Bay clergy.

In May 1743 the Congregational clergy of the province again assembled in Boston. By then, even Awakening proponents realized that itineracy and the attacks on the clergy had become a cancer eating at the heart of Massachusetts religious life. Chauncy became the strategist for the "Old Lights" and choreographed an effective, if hostile, opposition to the evangelicals in attendance. At one point he sought to quash efforts of revival backers to address the assembly for fear that their views would carry the day. Finally the ministers adopted a statement critical of Davenport's slurs on the clergy, but Chauncy refused to add his name to its list of endorsers because the document did not condemn the revivals in general.[39]

The General Court came to the aid of the frightened ministers by issuing a "presentment" against Davenport, accusing him of slander and reviling the clergy. But all these actions failed to end the religious strife. Although Davenport later retracted his attacks on the clergy, the people simply became more hardened in their support for, or opposition to, the revivals, and an era marked by splits in numerous congregations, several between "Old Lights" and "New Lights," began.[40]

Whitefield returned to Boston in 1744 and, albeit in a more responsible fashion, fed the doubts in people's minds about the Christian character of the clergy which Davenport had raised. Chauncy encountered Whitefield on the street one November day: " 'So you have returned, Dr. Whitefield, have you?' He replied, 'Yes, reverend Sir, in the service of the Lord.' 'I am sorry to hear it,' said Chauncy. 'So is the Devil!' was the answer given."[41] In an exchange of public letters with Whitefield, Chauncy condemned the evangelist for engaging in itinerant preaching and for questioning the authenticity of the religious experiences of the city's ministers.[42] Some contemporaries judged Chauncy as guilty of harsh judgment of others as he declared Whitefield to be. Thomas Prince, sympathetic to the evangelicals, wrote to Chauncy:

> In such a season as this should you rather not set a contrary example while you are publickly condemning such a spirit in others? Mr. Wh[itefield]. will hear you, but you will not hear him. Pray who appears most for separation or union? Methinks you should be glad of an occasion to show as good a Spirit as he.[43]

Chauncy issued one other vindication of the regular clergy in a sermon based on I Timothy 4:16: "Take heed unto thyself and unto the doctrine; continue in them; for in doing this thou shalt both save thyself, and them that hear thee."[44] He defended his belief in the positive instrumentality of even "unconverted" ministers on the grounds that since no human possessed full knowledge of the inward state of another, none could legitimately challenge the character of the clergy. In any case, he argued, the success of the gospel depended on the work of God, not on the state of the clergy's souls. Chauncy encouraged each minister to develop his peculiar gifts, although he suggested that most would be dependent on traditional patterns of clerical activity—ample study, lengthy sermon preparation time, and the like—for success. Indeed, he noted that cases in which ministers manifested extraordinary qualifications without following this routine were rare. He again decried doctrinal errors which he felt rampant during the revivals, singling out the necessity of assurance for special criticism.

While he joined the evangelicals in accenting the need for the inspiration of the Spirit if ministers were to be able to carry out the duties of their office, he cautioned against expecting the immediate influence of the Spirit in any situation. Just as the Spirit was more likely to come to individuals as they employed the traditional "means of grace" in seeking salvation than through the emotional excesses of the revivals, so it was more likely to empower the clergy as they worked diligently in their studies than as they spoke *ex tempore* in an effort to arouse the passions.

By the time the provincial clergy assembled for their 1744 convention, the wave of religious enthusiasm had crested. The "Old Lights," fearful of schisms in their own congregations, were securely in control. Chauncy was designated to preach to the gathered clergy. The title of his discourse reveals something of his mood: *Ministers Cautioned Against the Occasions of Contempt.*[45] Speaking as one who led the assault against those forces which sought to degrade the New England ministry, Chauncy exhorted his listeners to develop the traditional clerical virtues—study, exemplary moral conduct, responsible public activity, and the like—as effective means to ward off future attacks on the standing order. If the ministers themselves brought their lives and professional endeavors closer to the ideal, detractors would have little basis for complaint, and the ministry would be secure in its high status in New England life.

Chauncy's choice of ministerial deportment as his sermon theme reflected both his belief that attacks on the clergy remained the most reprehensible by-product of the Awakening and a continuing fear that such slurs would again shake the churches if the clergy did not take steps to protect their own interests. In any case, the address signalled the effective close of the general debates over the revivals; after 1744 the divisions between "Old Lights" and "New Lights" continued, but disputes became centered in individual towns rather than striking the entire colony.

In opposing the Awakening, Chauncy believed that he was defending the structures and symbols of order associated with the covenant tradition in a manner "seasonable" to the times. To an extent, the conflict between Chauncy and the evangelicals stemmed from different responses to a felt need to preserve the covenant heritage in a day when the homogeneity within New England society which once provided tacit support for the New England Way had collapsed. There was no longer a broad base of coherence which unified the people. Chauncy opted for preservation of the structures and symbols prompted by Puritan experience when he argued for the rational understanding of religious truth, for the validity of attendance on the "means of grace," and for the effectiveness and sanctity of the format of a settled clergy. If persons continued to place their hope of salvation in rational persuasion and adherence to the "means of grace" under the guidance of the clergy, covenant structures and symbols could continue to meet the religious needs of New England.

The evangelicals, however, opted to resuscitate what they believed to have been the kind of religious experience which gave birth to the covenant order. For them, if the primal experience could be regained, religious life would be revitalized. In this light, Chauncy stands as a conservative who realized that the use of reason, reliance on the "means of grace," and the model of a settled clergy were integral to the self-understanding of the community which stood in the heritage of the Puritan ideal. If these routes to salvation were discredited, that heritage would die. Conversely, if Puritanism were to live, its symbols and structures had to be protected and maintained. Chauncy became a spokesman for forces opposed to the evangelical Awakening because to do so was "seasonable" if one wanted to preserve the forms which had shaped New England religious life and to buttress the plausibility of the Puritan way.

Curiously, though, Chauncy has usually been seen as a liberal. This understanding of Chauncy's stance has its modern roots in the appraisal of Vernon L. Parrington, who was thoroughly captivated by the rationalistic tradition in American thought. Operating with the facile notion that rational equals liberal and believing that the liberal strand represented the mainstream of American intellectual history, Parrington cavalierly dismissed Jonathan Edwards as a reactionary and the Awakening as an anachronism. Correspondingly, those such as Chauncy, who opposed the revivals, became liberal heroes.[46] Perry Miller accepted Parrington's oversimplified liberal/conservative categorization, but argued that both Edwards's thinking and the revivals were far from anachronistic. Indeed, since for Miller the Awakening stood as a central event in the creation of the modern American mind, Edwards became a harbinger of modernity.[47] Miller's thesis was pushed to the extreme by his disciple, Alan Heimert, who vigorously asserted that the views of Edwards and the Awakeners represented the mainstream of American thought, while religious "liberals" such as Chauncy were the ones who were reactionary in attempting to maintain an outmoded New England way.[48]

What none of these students of the American mind recognized was that neither conservatives nor liberals were or are formed from a single mold. Rather, what seems to be liberal or conservative needs to be examined from the perspective of motivation, for what impels a person to adopt a particular line of thinking or course of action may well reveal more than the surface content of thought or apparent direction of conduct. And when one scrutinizes Chauncy's thought and action during the Awakening, one cannot escape the conclusion that his motivation was essentially conservative. Chauncy sought simply to restore traditional order to New England religious life and to reclaim a proper role for reason in the wake of the disarray wrought by the Awakening and the overemphasis on emotion which he saw perpetuated by the revivalists' stress on an affective experience of conversion.

Leading the opposition to the Awakening had consumed much of Chauncy's energy. While he had still found time in the midst of the upheaval to discharge such public duties as opening the town meeting with prayer and serving on a committee to inspect the public schools,[49] when the revivals waned he again assumed the traditional role of the New England parson—pastor to his congregation, minister at large, and student of theology. For slightly more than a decade he pursued these ordinary clerical tasks, but he was also, perhaps unwittingly, preparing for future controversy.

3.

A Pastoral Interlude

After the furor of the Awakening had died down, Chauncy returned to the life of the New England pastor and head of a now prominent Boston household. But if Chauncy withdrew from public controversy, he was far from inactive in Boston life and continued to speak his mind on matters of religious and political import. In many ways, the years between the debates over the Awakening and the Episcopal Controversy of the 1760s, when Chauncy would again represent a major strand of New England thought, were years in which the contours of his own thinking took firmer shape. Indeed, three themes emerge in his published sermons and public statements during this more quiet period of his life, themes which were both consistent with his opposition to the Awakening and omens of arguments to come: pride in a developing American self-consciousness, the need to maintain church order, and the preservation of Puritan theological categories while updating the content of Puritan thought.

When Chauncy commented on the various struggles which marked New England's participation in the continuing English conflict with the French for supremacy in eastern North America, he was quick to laud colonial wisdom and skill, grounding his praise in a recognition of a distinctively American nationalism and calling for an even stronger common identity among English colonists as Americans. The future strength of this now incipient American national identity would ultimately form one prop supporting Chauncy's endorsement of the move for independence from Britain. On those occasions when Chauncy addressed matters of particular concern to the clergy, as in his Election Sermon and his statements as a member of various church councils, he forcefully reiterated his commitment to the traditional religious order in New England. In the era of the Awakening, Chauncy had castigated the evangelical impulse largely because he saw it as a threat to the established religious structures which placed the clergy on a pedestal of respect and power. Now, too, he guarded against potential dangers to established church order by demanding better salaries for ministers and exonerating clergy facing dismissal from their pulpits when their doctrinal orthodoxy was challenged.

Chauncy always recoiled at any move which would weaken the formal structures which guarded New England religious life. And when he dabbled in theological writing in response to a pamphlet debate on the doctrine of original sin, Chauncy also revealed a pattern which would be operative until his death: he insisted on preserving the essential categories of Puritan thought even if modification in their interpretation was necessary to maintain their plausibility. In the midst of these years, somewhat removed from the limelight of public controversy, Chauncy himself labored on his own reinterpretation of Puritan theology, though he would not share his thinking openly until the last years of his life. But even then, Chauncy would want to claim that he set out to give renewed vigor to Puritan thought, not to destroy it, by bringing its content into harmony with the intellectual currents of the day while retaining its basic forms.

For the moment, though, Chauncy was content to devote himself to concerns within his family and to yield the public platform to his good friend, Jonathan Mayhew. Once the Awakening had ebbed, Chauncy found that his children and stepdaughter were pushing towards maturity, and it is likely that family responsibilities began to assume a goodly portion of the preacher's time.

Chauncy's one son became a particular problem for an orderly father. This son, also named Charles, had matriculated at Harvard in 1744, exploring collegiate life more exuberantly than had the now well-known pastor. Before the younger Charles's graduation in 1748 he had come to the attention of the college faculty as a trouble maker. In 1747 he was dropped six places in the class ranking for unauthorized possession of keys to several college rooms and denying that he had them. Although he was restored to his standing as second in the class before graduation, he was fined twice for violation of college rules, once for breaking into a closed study and once for making unnecessary noise.[1] Perhaps there was little question of the young graduate's following his father into the ministry, for after receiving his B.A. he settled in Kittery Point, New Hampshire, as an associate in the counting house of his uncle, Sir William Pepperrell. Finally he did develop that sense of discipline which Puritans saw as a prerequisite to success, for he became a prosperous New Hampshire merchant and in later years became active in the American movement for independence from Britain.

But Charles, Junior, was not the only member of the Chauncy household to reach adulthood as the revivals died out. On July 1, 1746, Rebecca Townshend, Mrs. Chauncy's daughter, married John Winthrop and moved to Cambridge where Winthrop, as Hollis professor of mathematics and natural philosophy, was making Harvard College one of the foremost centers of advanced scientific exploration and study in the colonies.

While Chauncy dealt with family concerns and carried on his pastoral duties, another younger Boston cleric, Jonathan Mayhew, was more than willing to don the mantle of public combat.[2] Son of Experience Mayhew, a missionary to the Indians on Martha's Vineyard, Jonathan entered Harvard in 1740 just as the Awakening erupted in New England. His intellectually formative period thus coincided with the turbulence of the revival years when queries were voiced in all quarters about the nature of the salvific experience and the role played by the individual in the process of salvation. Imbibing the heady wine of Enlightenment rationalism, Mayhew staunchly opposed the Awakening because to him its apparent emphasis on emotion and the affections insulted a human being's rational capacities. When Mayhew accepted a call to Boston's ten-year-old West Church in 1747, after its pastor, William Hooper, had sailed to England to secure Anglican orders, he found the city's clergy so suspicious of his doctrinal stance that most were unwilling to attend or participate in his ordination and, despite Chauncy's efforts in his behalf, continued to oppose his admission into the Boston Association of Ministers until his death.

Mayhew lost little time in confirming the fears of the more orthodox and in so doing took the heat off Chauncy as a radical firebrand promoting rationalistic religion. In 1749, Mayhew published a sermon entitled "The Right and Duty of Private Judgment" in which he articulated a rationalist approach to religious experience which made Chauncy's earlier stance seem middle of the road. Mayhew claimed that each individual must assume a position of indifference in religious matters in order to examine critically all religious truth claims, to weigh arguments for and against each point of view, and to be able to follow the truth wherever it was found, assenting to a stance in proportion to the degree of rational evidence in its behalf. This individual use of reason provided the only means to spiritual happiness, according to Mayhew, since each person framed religious questions in a unique way and therefore had to seek individual answers. Mayhew declared that authentic Christianity supported such rational pursuits since Christ had endowed humans with rational power as an integral dimension of their basic nature and along with his disciples had argued on rational grounds in his own ministry. All efforts to secure uniformity of belief or even to demand adherence to creeds refuted the essence of Christianity as a rational religion, but logic and persuasion could be employed to attempt to convince another of the truth of religion or of a particular religion.[3]

But what if the rational pursuit of truth led one to error? Mayhew responded to this possible dilemma in another sermon in which he revealed his unbounded confidence in human reason. The right of rational judgment did not grant one the liberty to choose error because the rational process itself would unveil error and demand that the individual reject it.[4] Of course, Mayhew no doubt personally believed that if everyone engaged in the sort of rational inquiry he proposed, all would reach conclusions substantially identical with his own. If he did not regard his personal position as the apex of religious truth, he was at least convinced that the truth would always be found in the Protestant rather than in the Roman Catholic tradition.[5] But Mayhew never countenanced the use of coercion to secure assent to any one position, and he recognized that the history of the Massachusetts Puritan commonwealth was not without its blemishes in this regard. In a 1754 sermon, for example, he pointedly asked whether the laws of the province with regard to dissenting groups resulted in religious persecution which was an abomination to both reason and the Christian religion.[6]

Earlier Mayhew had aroused considerable anguish among his peers when he took advantage of the official 1750 anniversary commemoration of the "martyrdom" of Charles I to preach a sermon arguing for the right of citizens to resist and overthrow tyrannical rulers. He began the discourse with a brief statement of the traditional Puritan belief in the divine sanction given to government as the vehicle for the ordering of society and extended to those who exercised authority within government. He quickly moved to a theoretical denial of the necessity or appropriateness of absolute obedience to any political authority, for he asserted that obedience was required only when rulers properly exercised the duties of their offices. When one who had been granted political power "turns tyrant and makes his subjects a prey to devour and to destroy instead of his charge to defend and cherish, we are bound to throw off our allegiance to him and to resist. . . ."[7] The resistance of the English Puritans to Charles I, predicated on the conviction that Charles sought to exercise tyrannical power, provided clear precedent in the Puritan tradition for Mayhew's stance.[8] He had, however, departed from that strain in Puritan thinking stretching back to Calvin which reluctantly endorsed resistance by formally constituted and acknowledged groups, for he declared that responsibility for determining whether a ruler acted consistently with the duties of his office fell to the people themselves. Unfortunately, he gave few clues as to how the people might make that determination.

With Mayhew at the center of the stage, Chauncy could readily afford to step aside. He remained Mayhew's close friend, probably because Mayhew was more open and more vociferous in articulating positions with which he was himself in basic agreement. As Conrad Wright ably appraised their relationship:

> . . . The two complemented one another well. Chauncy was solid, respectable, and careful not to allow his Arminianism to show too early or too conspicuously. Mayhew was temperamentally bolder and more forthright; with the support of his church behind him, he had no hesitation about saying quite bluntly the sort of thing that Chauncy would write down at length on paper and then set aside until the time was ripe for publication. In a sense, Chauncy influenced from within, while Mayhew goaded from without; under their combined influence, Boston merchants soon became accustomed to a liberal gospel.[9]

When Mayhew died in 1766, Chauncy preached the funeral sermon and found that the spotlight was again shining on him.

If Mayhew had somewhat imprudently drawn attention to

some of the problematic dimensions of a colonial relationship in his discourse on political resistance, Chauncy also directed some of his concern to public issues. After all, to stand in the Puritan heritage was to believe that history was the arena of divine activity *par excellence* and that political events did not transpire in random fashion, but according to God's purposes. In 1745–1746, the mother country was rocked by a military uprising in Scotland which was popularly believed to be part of a plot, organized with support from France and Spain, to place a Roman Catholic on the British throne. When the insurrection was quashed, Chauncy preached a sermon of thanksgiving. As a Protestant in the Calvinist tradition, Chauncy argued that Roman Catholicism was a natural enemy to true religion. His tone demonstrated even greater fear of possible Catholic expansion in the English Protestant world than he ever expressed towards the Church of England. Two factors prompted Chauncy's abhorrence of Rome: the heritage of severe repression of Protestants in Catholic countries and the legal relationship between Catholicism and government in those countries, as well as in the French and Spanish colonies in the New World, which meant that religious leaders could call upon the coercive power of the state to get their way. For Chauncy, popery was nothing less than slavery because it bound the individual to what he viewed as a rigid religious scheme and demanded unquestioning allegiance to the Pope on political and religious matters.

Chauncy discussed the recent threat to the English Protestant monarch on three levels.[10] First, although he repudiated the divine right theory of monarchy, he insisted that the king ruled with God's pleasure. Whatever government was established in a country operated with divine approval. Consequently, any attempt to overthrow the crown was by definition evil. Second, since the British monarchy had been in a Protestant succession from the time of the accession of William and Mary, Chauncy was certain that God would never permit a papist on the throne. Third, the present Hanoverian king,

George II, had never denied any the liberty to practice his or her own religion so long as that religion did not threaten the security of the political order. The same would not be true, Chauncy believed, if a Catholic were to reign. He assumed that a Catholic monarch would attempt to require all English people to adopt Roman faith and practice. In addition, current British policy permitted "true religion" to flourish in New England, a sure sign that God would not allow the monarchy to crumble. Indeed, Chauncy asserted, all English subjects on both sides of the Atlantic were now knit to the king because of their invaluable civil and religious privileges.[11] For him at this time, a threat to the monarchy was a threat to the New England Way.

The direct involvement of New England in this episode of intrigue had by and large been limited to an expedition against French-held Cape Breton Island in 1745. The colonial victory was hailed by Chauncy as the work of Providence, acting through Massachusetts troops as a secondary cause.[12] Chauncy's exuberance was also no doubt related to the fact that the Massachusetts regiment served under the command of his brother-in-law from his first marriage, Sir William Pepperrell, with whom he carried on an extensive correspondence during the conflict. It was also an occasion to demonstrate to the world that Americans had developed a high degree of military skill and were capable of defending their own interests.[13]

The New England Way, of course, had in its own fashion long regarded religion and politics as informally intertwined, since both were ostensibly ordained by God to advance the welfare of human beings. The close links between the two sectors are particularly evident in the phenomenon of the New England election sermon. At the time of the annual election in Massachusetts, a prominent clergyman was invited to preach at a service attended by the governor, the Council, and members of the lower house. Custom decreed the publication of the election sermons which, until the fervor of rebellion began to build in the 1760s and 1770s, usually consisted of an exhortation to the officials to fill their stations with due regard to their moral obligations and their responsibilities to God and to the citizenry. In 1747, when Chauncy received the honor of addressing the political powers of Massachusetts, he caused such a furor that questions were raised regarding the propriety of publishing his sermon.

The portion of the discourse which inflamed the legislators dealt with clerical salaries. Except in Boston, salaries of clergymen were fixed by the several towns and raised by taxation on all who could not offer proof of active membership in another legally recognized religious body. In areas where towns were not formally chartered, the General Court assumed responsibility for supervising the selection and payment of local religious teachers. Chauncy argued that the fixed clerical salaries, often paid in devalued currency rather than in sterling, needed adjustment because of inflation.[14] His point was no doubt valid, but it was regarded as a breach of etiquette and an intrusion on the legal prerogative of the legislature for a distinguished minister to address the law makers on matters of such seeming self-interest. When Chauncy learned that the General Court considered not publishing his sermon, he declared that it would appear in print regardless of the legislators' wishes. In a fit of non-Puritan anger, he blasted the Court: " 'And do you, Sir,' he added, 'say from me, that, if I wanted to initiate and instruct a person into all kinds of iniquity and double-dealing, I would send him to our General Court.' "[15]

In retrospect, that then sensational point of practical politics merits little attention, although it does indicate that Chauncy believed that the state had a proper concern for the general welfare of its citizens and especially of the clergy, who occupied a peculiar and prominent position in the Massachusetts social order. What is more important is the distinction Chauncy made between might and right, between just authority and tyranny, a distinction which should be joined with his exhortation to the governing powers to preserve the civil and religious liberties of the people.[16] If liberty were to exist in any sector, the boundaries of political authority had to be clearly delineated lest those who held power would seek self-aggrandizement at the expense of the people whose interests they supposedly guarded and promoted.

Chauncy declared that the civil realm had no jurisdiction to determine religious doctrine, but should allow each person to choose and practice his or her own religion as long as individual conduct in fulfilling religious obligations did not hinder public safety.[17] Chauncy no doubt had both Roman Catholicism and the Church of England in mind as possible threats to the New England scheme. If either gained political power, constituted authority would become tyranny, for Chauncy believed, as did Mayhew, that each would impose its religious patterns on the populace if it controlled the government. In an aside to William Shirley, the crown appointed governor, Chauncy expressed concern lest the governor trample on the accepted charter rights of the Massachusetts Puritans because his own religious allegiance was to a church which did not share the New England view of ecclesiastical structure or of church-state relations. He summarized these charter rights as the liberty to continue the New England pattern of assumed Congregationalist supremacy.[18] Chauncy's position was not without its logical foundation, for he and his Puritan compatriots did belong to a dissenting religious group, albeit the dominant religious body in Massachusetts, and possible control of governmental machinery by a hostile religious group could easily be interpreted as tyranny. But Chauncy never raised the question of whether the Congregationalists themselves were guilty of perpetrating a tyranny of the majority, a point to which Mayhew alluded and one which would soon be vigorously pressed by Isaac Backus, the Baptist spokesman.

When the decade of the 1740s closed, Chauncy was exhausted physically and intellectually. He reported to Pepperrell that he suffered from an "inveterate colick" which he could not shake.[19] In the eighteenth century, travel was considered a good remedy for minor sickness, so in May 1751 Chauncy set out in the company of Edward Jackson on a tour of the colonies. Their exact itinerary is unknown, but in March 1752 Chauncy was "reading" to a small congregation in Bath, North Carolina, returning to Boston by summer.[20] At once he resumed his wider pastoral duties, directing his attention both to the missionary ministry of the church and to the political responsibilities of the preacher.

Soon Chauncy was asked to participate in a special service to commission a missionary among the Indians. The failure of New England Christians to draw the native Indians into the fold of the elect had been a thorn in Puritan flesh almost from the inception of the Massachusetts enterprise.[21] Although few New Englanders felt called of God to devote their lives to Indian missions, whenever one did take up that vocation the devout would celebrate with a service of thanksgiving. Shortly after Chauncy returned to Boston, Gideon Hawley prepared to embark on a missionary career among the Indians in what is now upstate New York. A special service to set him apart for this high calling was held at Boston's First Church, with both Chauncy and Foxcroft participating. Before leaving for the wilds of the New York frontier, Hawley journeyed to Stockbridge for further theological study with Jonathan Edwards, now himself a missionary among the Indians since he had been dismissed from the Northampton pulpit.[22] It may seem curious that Hawley should first receive Chauncy's blessing and then sit at the feet of his Awakening foe, but the paradox is most likely resolved by the facts that the old controversy had by then virtually become a datum of history rather than a burning dispute and that all who stood in the Puritan heritage recognized the duty of spreading the gospel as an obligation which transcended theological differences.

Closer to home, other problems evoked responses from Chauncy. Boston, as the most populous city in the colonies, was experiencing a dilemma which continues to plague urban centers, the matter of burgeoning welfare rolls. Then as now, funds for the support of the unemployed were drawn from taxes which few were happy to pay. Some Boston citizens proposed to alleviate the situation by establishing a factory for the manufacture of linen and linen products. The factory would provide jobs for many of the unemployed and would thereby reduce the number of people on welfare. But British imperial policy forbade such colonial industry, requiring American subjects to purchase manufactured goods produced in the mother country. To endorse the linen factory proposal was, in a relatively minor way, to challenge the authority of Britain over her colonies. But it was also a challenge to the hegemony of Boston's import merchants over the city's economy, persons whose concerns Chauncy usually adopted as his own. Placing home manufactures on the market at lower prices than imported goods would cut into their trade.

Nevertheless, in a sermon on Christian charity Chauncy indirectly attacked both British policy and local economic interests. He enthusiastically endorsed the proposal, arguing that since the factory would provide jobs for welfare persons who were physically able to work, it would leave only the hopelessly disabled, the true objects of Christian charity, dependent on public support.[23] In reply to criticism anticipated from Boston importers, Chauncy simply declared that those afraid of colonial industry's potential damage to trade were acting from selfish motives and not from concern for the whole society. Alan Heimert correctly interpreted Chauncy's move when he suggested that Chauncy probably regarded the linen factory proposal not so much as a speculative business enterprise, but as an "investment" in furthering domestic tranquility.[24] By providing jobs and thereby keeping the people busy, the plan would halt what was perceived to be a growing problem of moral disorder in Boston, and by reducing the amount of welfare subsidy needed, it would ultimately benefit those from whose pocketbooks taxes were paid to support the poor.

Chauncy plainly did not view the industrial scheme as a

move towards a classless society. As an heir to Calvin, he believed that each individual had a proper calling to fulfill in this life, and he accordingly attached a positive value to work. Natural law convinced him that humans could not survive without labor; Scripture decreed that God made labor one component of the human situation after the Fall; history demonstrated that no society flourished without diligent labor on the part of its members; and reason made apparent the necessity of labor to tap the resources of the land.[25] Idleness, therefore, was the calling of none, especially not of the poor. But Chauncy did assert that the wealthy had some right to "exempt themselves from the lower and more servile Parts of Business."[26] Twenty years later, he echoed this theme when he declared that human society would always be composed of both the rich and the poor, that social and economic levelism was "an absurdity in reason," and that encouragement of individual initiative in acts of charity was the proper expression of Christian love.[27]

Chauncy's economic advice to the citizens of Boston contained three important implications. The first is the corollary to the earlier denial of the right of political government to determine the content of religious belief and practice: the church had not only the right, but the duty to suggest to the political realm business programs and policies which were intended to promote the establishment of a society whose principles were consonant with and supportive of right doctrine, especially when that doctrine itself undergirded the rationale for government's existence. The linen factory, by providing jobs, would both reinforce the positive value New England Puritans attached to work and advance the welfare of the whole society, the chief concern of government. Second, no one had the right or liberty to be economically lazy and to expect the civil order to care for one's personal needs. Christian charity and responsible government both decreed that the state should make opportunities for work available, not that it should provide for those who refused to labor on their own behalf. Finally, even if correct action in the political realm impinged on the economic prosperity of the wealthy, as the establishment of a linen factory might have done, the wealthy, by virtue of their position in society, did have greater liberty to pursue their own peculiar interests. It was therefore the duty of the civil government simultaneously to provide employment opportunities for the poor, enabling them to become productive members of society, and to protect as much as possible the economic liberty of the wealthy to use the advantages gained by their success as long as they kept the welfare of the whole society in view.

Although the linen factory never got off the ground, Chauncy's interest in Boston affairs did not diminish. In both 1754 and 1761 he served on town committees to inspect the public schools and report to the Selectmen on educational conditions in the city; and on March 11, 1754, and again on March 8, 1762, he offered the opening prayer at the Boston town meeting.[28] Chauncy took advantage of one event in the public sector to indulge in some old-fashioned Puritan moral instruction. On November 28, 1754, William Wieer was to be publicly executed for the murder of William Chism. From his pulpit at Old Brick that same day Chauncy delivered a sermon entitled *The Horrid Nature, and Enormous Guilt of Murder.*[29] Advocating capital punishment as the divinely ordained sentence for murder, Chauncy argued that murder was hateful to humanity and to God, using both rational and religious "proofs" to make his point. Murder was shocking to the human mind because it manifested a "high degree" of uncharitableness, a pleasant euphemism for antisocial conduct, on the part of the murderer in denying to another opportunity for the full pursuit of earthly happiness. More importantly, the perpetrator of murder usurped God's role as sovereign of the universe and ultimate giver of life. Such audacity constituted a religious crime worthy of damnation itself. So heinous was murder in Chauncy's mind that he forbade his listeners to have pity on the criminal who, after all, had received a fair trial and would in death, at least, have no more temptation to sin. The rigidity of Chauncy's belief that capital punishment was an appropriate response to "horrid" crime moved one later commentator to remark that had Chauncy lived in a different age he no doubt would have eagerly had religious heretics burned at the stake.[30]

One other occurrence—an earthquake which shook Massachusetts on November 18, 1755—offered Chauncy the opportunity for Puritan moralizing. Declaring that earthquakes usually testified to the wrath of God towards a sinful people, Chauncy catalogued the shortcomings he observed around him: the prevalence of sexual licentiousness in Boston, failure to observe the Sabbath with due solemnity, wanton drunkenness and revelry, dishonest commercial practices such as price fixing, inordinate human pride, and blatant disregard for Christ and the church. As Puritan preachers for nearly two centuries had exhorted their constituents, Chauncy called upon his people to repent and return to the righteousness their ancestors had demonstrated in leading godly lives.[31]

Other events in 1755 forced Chauncy to broaden his vision from Boston to the whole of New England, for that year also witnessed the outbreak of military conflict with the French which did not end officially until the Peace of Paris was signed in 1763 and the French had been virtually eliminated from North America. General Braddock had arrived in the colonies in 1754 as commander-in-chief of the royal forces, bringing two regiments of British Regulars with him, and the following year he set out to destroy the French outpost at Fort Duquesne. His utter defeat and the consequent, though momentary, humiliation of the British and American troops brought an "open letter" from Chauncy. In it, Chauncy offered a glimpse of his later attitude towards the justice of America's colonial relationship with England.[32]

After chastising the southern colonies for their failure to provide fighting men, he heaped criticism on the British. He did not question Braddock's ability as a general, but sharply challenged whether any of the British army knew the best techniques for conducting a war on American soil in the wilderness. The Boston divine then declared that Braddock would not have been defeated if he had solicited and followed the advice of the American soldiers. Indeed, he suggested that to win an American war, American militia were needed as much as the British Regulars. And since American forces were indispensible to victory, Chauncy objected to the policy of granting British officers superiority over Americans of the same rank. As Richard Slotkin has observed, Chauncy argued that Braddock's defeat dramatically demonstrated the need for a greater assertion of national pride in a distinctively American identity, for Chauncy saw New England's experience as representative of the experience of all the American colonies.[33]

In an aside in his "letter," he endorsed the controversial 1754 Albany Plan of Union, drafted primarily by Benjamin Franklin and Massachusetts' Thomas Hutchinson, because he believed that such a confederation would provide appropriate recognition of the political maturity of the colonies and their intertwined interests. He closed the tract with an appeal for financial help from Britain to ease the colonial burden in carrying on the war, though he acknowledged that there was no historical precedent for such monetary subsidy.

When the combined British and American forces defeated the French at Lake George later that year, Chauncy felt that the truth of his earlier arguments had been plainly demonstrated. In another "letter to a friend," he attributed the success largely to the fact that the British troops had started to fight like Americans. The victory was significant both because it removed the disgrace of the Ohio defeat and because it had greatly weakened the enemy. According to Chauncy, Massachusetts men had comprised the largest segment of the combined British and American army, and Massachusetts had also provided the most substantial monetary support for the venture. But an expression of pride in his colony was not his only motive in singling out Massachusetts' contributions to the war effort. He renewed his plea for financial assistance from Britain, claiming that the province stood on the brink of economic collapse unless help were forthcoming and that Massachusetts' role in the engagement made the colony deserving of monetary aid.[34]

In these two pamphlets, Chauncy provided several clues about his developing political position. Clearly he felt that the colonies should exercise a large degree of responsibility in determining their own affairs. His emphasis on the value of American military wisdom and leadership in directing a war on American soil signalled his increasing belief in the justice of giving the colonists a free hand in the conduct of the conflict because they knew the American situation better than the British. And while he admitted that Americans should assume a substantial share of the cost of the operation, he insisted that Great Britain should subsidize the undertaking because of the strategic importance of the war to the security of the mother country. Chauncy was simply indicating that the colonies knew what they were about and deserved the liberty to guide their own affairs. A colonial relationship in his mind did not signify the subservience and deference of colony to mother country, but mutual aid and support between them in times of need.

But Chauncy, the Puritan preacher, was not content to lay all blame for America's woes at the hands of the British. In his Boston Thursday lecture presented January 22, 1756, he joined together the destruction wrought by the recent earthquake and the war with the French and Indians in a jeremiad bemoaning the religious laxity of his peers. While he insisted that suffering had been integral to the human situation since the Fall, he also declared that the extent of suffering experienced at any given time was contingent on the degree of sin prevalent among the people. Hence if the Boston citizenry wished to avoid the devastation of earthquakes, the miseries of war, and the injustices of British military policy, they should once again make religion the "grand care" of their lives.[35]

Theological study absorbed much of Chauncy's personal

interest during this period when he was less conspicuously in the public eye than he had been during the Awakening years. Although he continued to read the standard Puritan authorities, especially Richard Baxter, he was increasingly drawn to contemporary theological literature and current theological discussion. Chauncy always found the life of the pastor-scholar appealing and thrived on those hours when he could be alone poring over theological treatises and the Scriptures. The theological debates of the 1750s were primarily intramural in nature, which is to say that they aroused the clergy more than they caught the fancy of the people. The particular dogma which troubled theological waters in that era was the doctrine of original sin.

The discussion opened when colonials began serious reading of a treatise by John Taylor, a dissenter of pronounced Arminian sympathies from Norwich, England. Entitled *The Scripture Doctrine of Original Sin, Proposed to a Free and Candid Examination,* the work had appeared in Britain in the 1740s but did not gain a wide American readership until after the Awakening had subsided.[36] Taylor and those who supported his position were distressed by two corollaries to the orthodox explication of original sin. Taylor never questioned the actual sinfulness of humanity, but he did have qualms about the Calvinist notions of imputed guilt and total depravity. On the one hand, it seemed irrational to suggest that Adam's sin was transferred to the whole of the human race. Logically Taylor felt that one could be held responsible only for one's own actions; hence a gracious God could not hold Adam's posterity liable for the sins of the first man. On the other hand, the usual statement of total depravity as a denial of any positive human capacities seemed to Taylor to denigrate human integrity and render salvation meaningless if not impossible. It followed in his mind that if depravity left no point of contact between the human and the divine, not even the Incarnation could bridge the gap. Total depravity thus destroyed the heart of the Christian message.

For the moment the content of Taylor's critique attracted less attention than the method of Scriptural analysis he had used to arrive at his conclusions. Writing to his cousin, Nathaniel Chauncey, on April 14, 1754, Chauncy dismissed the content while expressing appreciation for the method: "I am without all doubt, that Mr. Taylor for whom I have a great value, and to whom I am much beholden, is very much mistaken in his doctrine of original sin. . . ."[37] What made Chauncy "beholden" to Taylor was the latter's format of comparing every biblical text on a specific topic, paraphrasing awkwardly translated passages, and returning to the original language of a text to determine nuances of particular words before attempting an explication of a particular doctrine. While these methodological tools were neither unique to Taylor nor first developed by him, they did become popular in America through his writings. Chauncy, for one, was particularly captivated by Taylor's approach and began to explore a wide range of doctrinal issues using it. The results of his sustained inquiry were ultimately to lead him to refashion much of the Puritan theology he inherited. But for the time being he left his conclusions in manuscript form, referring to them collectively as "the pudding." He did discuss his reformulated views with selected associates, but remained content to wait for a "seasonable" time to release "the pudding" to the public.

The investigation into the meaning of original sin gained momentum. In 1757 Samuel Webster, pastor at Salisbury, Massachusetts, published *A Winter Evening's Conversation upon the Doctrine of Original Sin* in which he vigorously advanced Taylor's position.[38] It was one thing for an heir of Puritanism to find Taylor's Scriptural methods useful; it was another, more serious matter to have an advocate of his unorthodox theology preaching and publishing in Massachusetts. Jonathan Edwards, still "in exile" in Stockbridge, had drafted a stinging reply to Taylor, defending what he regarded as the orthodox Calvinist position. While it had been completed beforehand, the work appeared after Webster's monograph was off the press.[39] The "Old Lights," however, were unwilling to have their former foe lead their rebuttal, despite his creative and original effort to buttress the idea of imputed guilt. Edwards used Locke's understanding of personal identity to advance a doctrine of the continuous re-creation of the world which made each person one with Adam at every moment and therefore liable for Adam's sin.

Peter Clark, settled at the First Church in Salem Village (now Danvers), Massachusetts, took up the cudgels to defend orthodoxy from a more moderate stance.[40] When Chauncy examined Clark's work, he realized that instead of rebutting Webster and Taylor, Clark had given them more ammunition, for he had exposed a vulnerable point in the Calvinist scheme when he questioned whether infants who died before reaching the age of accountability would reap eternal damnation because of their supposed original sin. Chauncy was aware that denial of the eternal punishment of infants would remove a major prop buttressing the orthodox conception of original sin and therefore plunged into the fray with a brief essay in response to Clark. Instead of ripping apart Clark's views as he ostensibly intended, he wound up in basic agreement with Clark's refusal to accept the liability of infants to eternal punishment, for he found the idea of the damnation of infants repugnant to reason and experience.[41]

Chauncy may have been as surprised as his readers at his own conclusion, but he also realized what was at stake if one followed Clark's reasoning to its limits: the entire Calvinist theological structure would collapse.[42] Reinterpretation of doctrine was one matter; demolishing the theological underpinnings of New England religious thought was another. The first was acceptable as an avenue to preserve the plausibility of New England religious life; the latter would never do, for it would cause religious disorder of the worst sort. Chauncy quickly retreated to his study for further reflection. He was simply not yet prepared to undercut the content of that tradition which he believed he had successfully defended in the Great Awakening. After all, in his 1756 Thursday lecture he had mustered a more orthodox interpretation of original sin to reinforce his claim that suffering was intrinsic to the condition of fallen humanity.[43]

Along with his continuing theological inquiry, Chauncy carried out many tasks routinely incumbent upon a New England pastor. While his goals in pastoral leadership, as in theological disputes, remained essentially conservative, Chauncy was willing to tamper with peripheral matters if alternatives would allow the traditional ministry of a gathered congregation to meet new challenges. Under his leadership, several changes did transpire at Old Brick. In 1758, with Chauncy's approval, the congregation broke with Puritan precedent by organizing a choir.[44] The following year when a serious fire left sections of Boston in ashes, Old Brick, with some prodding from its junior minister, headed the list of contributors to the public relief fund.[45] The pastor's broader responsibility for the religious welfare of individuals and for the health of other congregations likewise commanded some of Chauncy's time. In 1752, for example, he assumed the role of marriage counselor in a dispute between Sampson and Margaret Stoddard. Nine years later, he sought with the aid of his friend, Ezra Stiles, to mediate in a financial quarrel between a man in Boston and a citizen of Newport, Rhode Island.[46]

Chauncy was also drawn into the ecclesiastical morass surrounding the dismissal of the Reverend John Rogers from the church at Leominster.[47] On the basis of several sermons, delivered in 1756 and 1757, which were Arminian in tone, the congregation called a council to appraise the theological orthodoxy of their pastor. When the council discovered that Rogers supported Webster's views on original sin and articulated a Christology which seemed to question the divinity of Christ, they recommended his dismissal. Chauncy then joined with his ideological allies Jonathan Mayhew and Ebenezer Gay on a rival council which concluded that there were no grounds for formal dismissal. Since his own stance was in flux, Chauncy's participation in this dispute probably stemmed less from a desire to endorse Rogers's theological position than it did from a firm conviction, going back to his defense of the standing order in the Awakening era, that all duly ordained ministers, regardless of their personal opinions, were vehicles through which God worked and should be accorded the respect attendant on that high status.

Chauncy had for some years maintained an extensive correspondence with Ezra Stiles, pastor in Newport and later president of Yale College. In 1761 he demonstrated his friendship by arranging for the publication of a volume of sermons by Stiles.[48] At the same time, Chauncy remained an involved member of the Harvard Board of Overseers, always eager to enhance the stature of his alma mater. When Eleazar Wheelock, commissioned as a missionary to the Indians in New Hampshire, sought to secure funds to establish an Indian school, Chauncy immediately recognized a threat to Harvard. He was partially correct, for Wheelock's Indian school developed into Dartmouth College, but he may have unjustly suggested that Wheelock was misusing funds which he had obtained for missions work. Convinced that missions money was making its way into the Dartmouth treasury, Chauncy struggled, probably unnecessarily, to get money from the estate of Sir Peter Warren donated to Harvard. Wheelock, of course, wanted the funds for his own enterprise.[49] Chauncy had further—and more legitimate—occasion to manifest his devotion to his college when Harvard Hall was destroyed by fire on January 24, 1764, for he then worked industriously on an Overseers' committee charged with raising funds for rebuilding the structure and replacing books and materials lost.[50]

While involved with these forays into Harvard affairs, the colony's politics, and changes at Old Brick, Chauncy had to deal with serious personal matters. In 1757, two momentous events occurred within the Chauncy family circle, one an occasion for rejoicing and one a time for mourning. That year,

Chauncy's daughter, Elizabeth, became the wife of Benjamin Greenleaf. Greenleaf was a prosperous young merchant in Newburyport and later an American patriot. After her marriage, Elizabeth Chauncy Greenleaf took up duties as mistress of her home in Newburyport, remaining there until her death in 1769. But on April 11, 1757, Chauncy's wife died, leaving him a widower for the second time. As before, Chauncy felt an acute need for wifely companionship, and on June 15, 1760, he married Mary Stoddard, a distant relative of Jonathan Edwards. Again marriage boosted Chauncy's social status, for the third Mrs. Chauncy was a woman of means, owning one-third of Noddle's Island and part interest in a sugar plantation in Antigua.[51] Chauncy now not only served Boston's premier congregation but was also advancing in the ranks of the Boston social hierarchy.

By and large, though, the decade or so after the Awakening had allowed Chauncy to live the ordinary life of the New England preacher and family man. But the 1760s were to thrust him once more into the thick of controversy. When he delivered the prestigious Dudleian Lecture at Harvard in 1762 on the validity of ordination by presbyters, the interlude was nearing an end.

4.

No Taxes, No Bishops

Once England had virtually obliterated the French presence in North America, she entered a brief period of military security which allowed government leaders to focus attention on the country's staggering war debt, its precarious economy, and the costs involved in administering an expanded colonial empire. The most pressing concerns shared at least one common ingredient: they all involved money and indicated that England required more funds in the government coffers. Taxation immediately presented itself as an obvious remedy to the problem. Accordingly, Parliament in 1765 enacted that legislation which ever after became known as the Stamp Act.

In the American colonies the legislation generated much hostility towards Britain, a hostility which stemmed as much from the popular belief that payment of the tax signalled impending economic ruin for the colonies as from the conviction that the law was but the first step in instituting a repressive colonial policy designed to end whatever control the colonies exercised over their own affairs and bring them finally under the wings of a tyrannical Parliament. Indeed, the principle behind the tax sparked a substantial outburst of protest. The issue, simply stated, was the fact that the colonies had been taxed by a legislative body in which they had no direct representation. The business of representation was confusing, in part because colonists had long acknowledged some Parliamentary authority over commercial activity in the levying of import and export duties. The literature sparked by the controversy centered on three specific points: a hypothetical distinction between internal and external taxes, the matter of taxation for revenue, and the nature of Parliamentary authority over the colonies in general.

Some colonial thinkers attempted to distinguish between two types of taxation: internal and external.[1] External taxes included such levies as the import-export duties which had been on the books for years, although haphazardly enforced. Since these duties were officially collected outside the colonies —import duties, for example, were paid before goods were unloaded in colonial ports—they properly fell under Parliamentary control. Internal taxes were those such as the stamp duty, levied inside the colonies and paid by the colonists directly. Persons who made the internal-external distinction saw internal taxation to be under the exclusive jurisdiction of the colonial legislative assemblies. But there was a fundamental fallacy in this line of reasoning: in the last analysis the colonists themselves were paying both types of taxes. If Parliament could legitimately levy one kind of tax on the colonies, could it not levy both?

The question of whether Parliament could tax in order to provide government revenue was another way to frame the same query. John Dickinson, for example, noted that before the 1760s Parliament had never enacted a colonial statute for the sole purpose of raising money to finance the operations of the English government.[2] To maintain the connections of empire for the supposed benefit of all was one matter; to tax a few for the benefit of a different few was quite another.[3] Few colonial thinkers at first acknowledged what later became apparent: trade duties also provided a revenue, small though it might have been, and if production of revenue by levies was the criterion for measuring the validity of taxes laid by Parliament, then commercial taxes fell into the same category as the stamp tax. John Dickinson did draw this conclusion, although he did not develop the idea fully at the time, when he questioned whether Parliament could legitimately tax products which the colonists were obliged to purchase from Britain alone.[4] Daniel Dulaney of Maryland, who wrote extensively in protest of the Stamp Act, noted that there were theoretical precedents for Parliament's claim to have the power of levying taxes for revenue, but that in earlier periods Parliament merely apportioned to the colonies certain amounts for designated purposes and allowed the colonial legislatures to set up ways to raise the money needed. He too saw the policy of the 1760s as a breach with past practice and not to be condoned.[5]

The heart of the matter, really, was determining whether Parliament held any authority to legislate for the colonies. James Otis, whose views on Parliamentary power were somewhat ambiguous, at one point acknowledged the right of Parliament to tax the colonies internally as well as externally and to tax in order to raise a revenue, but he believed that if Parliament exercised that power, it did so unjustly since the colonists had no elected representatives in Parliament who could symbolize their consent to taxation. He suggested that since the colonial legislatures already levied taxes in their own names, Parliament ought to refrain from exercising its power lest the colonies be taxed by two different bodies.[6] After all, residents of England were subject to taxation by only one legislative body, Parliament, to which they elected their own representatives. Few colonists ever bought the idea of "virtual representation," the notion that since every member of Parliament theoretically represented all British subjects as well as a particular constituency, colonists were already technically ("virtually") represented since they were subjects.

Massachusetts Governor Bernard recognized that the real issue was whether the colonists recognized any Parliamentary authority in fact, although they claimed to do so in theory.[7] Dulaney had insisted that all the colonists demanded as British subjects was "the right of exemption from all taxes *without their consent.*"[8] Bernard's point was that the taxation discussion symbolized far more than "no taxation without representation." Rather, the taxation controversies were a disguise for a more serious debate over whether the colonists were in any way subject to the legislative power of Parliament, particularly if that power were actualized in laws which the colonists did not like.

As dissatisfaction with the Stamp Act mushroomed and boycotts of British goods were organized, the Massachusetts General Court called for delegates from all the colonies to meet and develop a common course of action. Representatives from nine colonies gathered in New York in October 1765, forming what has since been called the Stamp Act Congress. The resolutions adopted fixed the issue of representation as primary. But before the congress had even convened, there had been a shift of power in England. In March 1766, the new Whig government succeeded in having Parliament repeal the odious legislation. When news of repeal reached the colonies, days of thanksgiving were proclaimed. In Massachusetts, people flocked to the churches to celebrate their victory. The content of the discourses delivered by the clergy discloses the depth of colonial sentiment against the tax.

The title of Jonathan Mayhew's sermon on that occasion, *The Snare Broken,* readily reveals his position. The stamp tax was a noose which would have strangled colonial liberties if it had been enforced. Yet, Mayhew asserted, the English heritage of liberty had given birth to a system of government which gave the colonies such an advantage in freedom over other nations that misfortune would have resulted if the dispute permanently weakened ties with the mother country. But the crisis had taught everyone the necessity of guarding against potential threats to liberty; the Stamp Act and consequent events were examples for the future.[9] Joseph Emerson, pastor at Pepperell, spoke more strongly when he declared that repeal was nothing less than deliverance from slavery.[10] Using the jeremiad form to suggest that a lack of a spirit of thankfulness to God for victory over the French and Indians had led to the passage of the Stamp Act, Emerson tied taxation by Parliament to an invasion of the charter rights of the colonies, including the right to taxation by elected representatives of the people.

He saw the move as setting a precedent which, unless halted, would ultimately lead to the loss of all colonial liberties, the most important of which was the liberty for Puritan religious institutions to flourish. If Parliament could tax, it could also formally establish the Church of England in the colonies, which in turn would seek to destroy "true religion."

Charles Chauncy also took to his pulpit to lead First Church parishioners in their service of thanksgiving. In his sermon he outlined four reasons why colonists should rejoice at the repeal of the Stamp Act. First, the repeal reflected "the kind and righteous regard the supreme authority in England, to which we inviolably owe submission, had paid to the 'commercial good' of the Nation at home, and its dependent provinces and Islands."[11] Removal of the tax insured the continuing prosperity of British colonial trade and strengthened colonial allegiance to the crown. The second cause for celebration was the withdrawal of the "grievous burden" of the tax itself. Chauncy insisted, perhaps naively, that the colonists' financial resources could support the paper tax for two years at most, since continuing payments on debts incurred in the Seven Years' War and prohibitions against printing new paper currency had made money unusually scarce.[12] Third, repeal renewed hope for further "enjoyment of certain liberties and privileges, valued by us next to life itself."[13] These liberties primarily concerned the degree of internal self-government which had developed in the colonies over the years and which many colonists thought was grounded in the colonial charters.

Chauncy did note that on technical and legal grounds the charters may not have authorized the extent of domestic self-government which many assumed as a basic right. Regardless, he argued, since these "liberties and privileges" were now enjoyed *de facto,* they should not be removed or reduced.

Finally, repeal restored the feeling of mutual love which the colonists shared with citizens in England as subjects of the same sovereign. Chauncy then contrasted the current state of happiness in the colonies with what might have ensued had the Stamp Act remained on the books. In his estimation, resistance clearly would have followed execution of the bill, and war might have ultimately accompanied its enforcement. But resistance to the tax, he asserted, was not a move to alter the colonial status of America. On the contrary, the "wiser sons of liberty" entertained no such thoughts. Rather, within the "bounds of a decent warrantable regularity"—petition and protest—they had sought to defend and secure the rights of the colonists as British subjects.[14]

At this time, then, Chauncy hardly sanctioned armed rebellion as a viable means of defending the colonists' presumed political prerogatives. His opposition to the Stamp Act represented an effort to maintain intact the structures of political authority which he believed had been operative prior to its passage. It was not a move to substitute a new system of government for the then current model, but one designed to preserve the system which he felt had governed colonial life before the rupture which had followed the last of the French and Indian Wars. Chauncy remained confident that Parliament would always respond to rational argument when the colonies sought to persuade policy-makers that certain programs were unwise. After all, just such rational persuasion had brought the desired result in the repeal of the Stamp Act. Again, a conservative approach struck Chauncy as the best guide to action. As long as ways sanctioned by tradition were effective, Chauncy refused to endorse alternative methods to challenge Parliamentary decisions. He simply wanted the pre-Stamp Act ethos restored with as little disruption of social order as possible. Chauncy's position was echoed by Andrew Eliot, one of the liberal clergy whose influential role on the Harvard Board of Overseers was regarded as paving the way for the later Unitarian ascendancy at that university. Eliot wrote to Harvard benefactor Thomas Hollis that Stamp Act resistance was not a call to independence, but an effort to regain lost liberties.[15]

Alan Heimert has castigated Chauncy for being too cautious in his Stamp Act repeal message since he did not insist that those charter rights which the colonists thought were theirs really belonged to them, but admitted that a legitimate case might be made that the powers in question were legally not theirs. Heimert believes that Chauncy should have made a firm case for the legal right of the colonies to total self-government.[16] Chauncy, however, did not approach the situation with Heimert's hindsight or with his passion for promoting eighteenth century evangelicalism as a major source of the ideology of political independence in the colonies. To Chauncy, whether the right to extensive self-government belonged to the colonies was not the issue at stake. He simply sought the restoration of what he believed to have been once operative patterns of political authority, patterns which assumed that the colonies did have the liberty to determine at least the domestic aspects of their common life. Chauncy spoke out in support of that scheme of things which promoted the maintenance of what he perhaps romantically viewed as a tranquil *status quo ante.* Possession of the right to domestic self-control was taken for granted. When Chauncy did criticize the British government for passing the Stamp Act, it was "seasonable" to do so because of the threat the Act supposedly rendered to established political practice.

The rejoicing over repeal was short-lived in religious circles. On the heels of the turmoil wrought by the Stamp Act crisis came a jolt to the ecclesiastical structures of New England. It appeared that plans were again underway to settle a Church of England bishop in America.[17] The controversy which ensued was one of those emotion-charged disputes which consumed far more time and energy among participants than the issue warranted. Within New England Congregationalism there had long been an aversion to the episcopal form of church government. In the early years of colonial settlement, Cotton Mather had expressed the commonly held Puritan view when he quoted an unidentified sermon:

> "Let all mankind know that we came into the *wilderness*, because we would worship God without that *Episcopacy*, that *common-prayer*, and those unwarrantable *ceremonies*, with which *the land of our fore fathers' sepulchres* has been defiled; we came because we would have our posterity settled under the pure *dispensations* of the gospel, defended *by rulers that should be of ourselves*."[18]

As early as 1638 Archbishop Laud outlined plans to send a bishop to New England but quickly abandoned them because of the trouble at home which led to the English Civil War, and serious thought about an American bishop then lay fallow until the close of the Seven Years' War a century and a quarter later.[19]

By the 1760s the situation was more complex and delicate than in the days of Laud because of two specific incidents in which Church of England bishops had induced the British government to interfere in the religious life of New England. In 1725 an attempt by Massachusetts Congregationalists to have the colony's Council officially recognize their synod was thwarted by the English government under pressure from both Church of England clergy in Boston and the Bishop of London, whose see included the colonies. Such recognition was regarded as a challenge to the status of the established church. Then in 1762 efforts to procure a charter for a Congregationalist sponsored Society for the Promotion of Christian Knowledge among the Indians were blocked by "the King in Council" after the Massachusetts Anglican clergy and Anglican missionaries to the Indians insisted that such an organization would hinder the ongoing work of the Church of England's Society for the Propagation of the Gospel among New England Indians.[20]

The task of stating New England's position originally fell to the outspoken Jonathan Mayhew. But Mayhew died in 1766 in the heat of controversy, leaving dissenters without a voice. While the Congregationalists waited to see who would assume Mayhew's defensive role, the agitation was intensified by the slurs cast on New England religious life in a sermon delivered by the Bishop of Landaff at the anniversary meeting of the S.P.G. The bishop claimed that colonial religion was deficient in its nature and negligent in carrying out its responsibility to convert the Indians. Establishing an American bishopric would help resolve the first problem by providing what Anglicans believed to be the proper ecclesiastical structure, and a stepped-up program under the aegis of the S.P.G. could deal with the second. Andrew Eliot drafted a reply to Landaff and asked Chauncy to read and comment on it before it went to press. To Eliot's surprise, Chauncy penned his own response and published it before Eliot had a chance to make his work public.[21]

Chauncy became such a vigorous defender of the Congregational Way that few of his compatriots bothered to enter the controversy directly. Some ultimately thought that Chauncy had unfairly pre-empted others and made it impossible for his colleagues to offer their own apology for New England polity.[22] But Chauncy's eagerness to join in this ecclesiastical combat should not have surprised his associates. After all, he had devoted considerable study to polity issues years before when his brother-in-law became an Anglican priest; his Dudleian Lecture at Harvard in 1762 had focused on the validity of ordination by "presbyters," and he had for several years corresponded with Micaiah Towgood, an Exeter, England, dissenting clergyman whose *High-Flown Episcopal and Priestly Claims Freely Examined* (1737) had attracted his attention.[23]

Chauncy's reply to the Bishop of Landaff's sermon assumed that the negative appraisal of New England religion which it contained was a veiled proposal to establish the Church of England in the colonies. He supported his view by claiming that S.P.G. missionaries had not devoted their primary attention to seeking Indian converts, but to working in areas where Congregationalism had a firm foothold. To Chauncy, such a move smacked of the oppression the Congregationalists had sought to escape by coming to America: *"Liberty to worship God agreeably to the dictates of conscience* was the *grand motive* to their removal hither; and the *enjoyment of this liberty* at so great a distance from *oppressive power* was their support under heavier tryals than can easily be conceived of by those who have never been in a wilderness country."[24]

If one recalled the situation in England when Laud had attempted to snuff out dissenters, including the founders of New England, one could accurately surmise what would ultimately happen in the colonies. When he discussed the bishop's lament over the lack of an American episcopate, Chauncy sketched arguments which he would expand in later works.[25] He feared that bishops would seek to use their "superiority" as spokesmen of an officially recognized and government-sponsored church to influence colonial politics to the advantage of the Church of England and thus to the detriment of the Congregationalists. Chauncy then raised the question of financial support for an American bishop on two levels. First, he doubted whether the Church of England had sufficient numerical strength in the colonies to support a resident bishop without subsidy. Second, he noted that in the mother country, tax monies financed episcopacy. New England, he declared, would regard public taxation to support a Church of England bishop as an infringement on political and religious liberty.

Thomas Bradbury Chandler, the rector of St. John's Church in Elizabethtown, New Jersey, who later became an ardent Loyalist, was delegated by his fellow American priests to counter Chauncy. In an *Appeal to the Public,* he elaborated three fundamental reasons why a bishop had not yet been sent to the colonies:

1. In New England's early days, nearly all the settlers were dissenters; accordingly, no bishop had then been needed.

2. For several years the Anglican population of the colonies had been large enough to need the ministrations of a bishop in such matters as confirmation and ordination, but other more pressing concerns had prevented appropriate government action.
3. Even now the government believed it was proceeding with caution in order not to infringe on the liberties of colonial dissenters.[26]

Chandler introduced a new element in the dispute when he insisted that American Church of England bishops would have only spiritual and ecclesiastical responsibilities, and those over only their own clergy, not the laity. The routine civil functions which English bishops exercised, such as issuing marriage licenses, would be abandoned in the colonies. In addition, he denied that the Church of England intended to establish ecclesiastical courts, tithes, or any other religious taxes in the colonies.[27]

Chauncy's quick reply basically restated his earlier arguments. He did query, however, whether any Church of England bishop could ever have purely spiritual and ecclesiastical functions. Since the Church of England was established by law and the king was technically its supreme governor, bishops as crown appointees were by definition arms of the state. American bishops, as Anglican bishops without a civil link, would really be no bishops at all.[28] A promise that colonial bishops would have strictly ecclesiastical duties was no proof that the bishops themselves would not seek to extend their powers once on the job, a move likely to result in the introduction of the dreaded taxes for their support.[29] Speaking for all colonial dissenters, Chauncy wrote: "We desire no other liberty, than to be left unrestrained in the exercise of our religious principles, in so far as we are good members of society."[30]

Chandler provided his rejoinder the following year, but said nothing really new. He again denied that Anglican bishops in America would have any temporal powers and assured his opponents that no new tax would be levied for their support. The bishops would be subsidized by private donation. Hence no menace to the religious and political liberties of the colonies existed.[31] Chauncy's retort appeared in 1770. He devoted nearly one-third of this treatise to a history of episcopacy within the Church of England to show that episcopal consecration was not necessary for valid Anglican ordination.[32] Anglican clergy in the colonies, therefore, did not even need a bishop with purely ecclesiastical responsibilities. He naively suggested that if episcopal consecration was desirable, it could be administered to American candidates by the Roman Catholic bishop in Canada or by the Moravian bishop in Pennsylvania.[33] He still maintained that the ultimate intention of the plan was to episcopize the colonies.

One more exchange followed before the debate closed. In his final contribution, Chandler asserted that Chauncy must really approve of the establishment of an American episcopate since his objections all referred to the possible civil authority of bishops which had already been discarded from the plan. He noted with pride the increasing support the proposal had garnered, not only among those Church of England laity who had formerly expressed some misgivings themselves, but also among Quakers and Baptists (who no doubt hoped that an Anglican bishopric would weaken Congregationalist "tyranny").[34]

Chauncy concluded his part in the debate when he decided the time was finally "seasonable" to offer his earlier tome on episcopacy to the public. Accordingly, in 1771 he succeeded in publishing the manuscript he had set aside in 1734 when he could not secure subscribers for it. Always the conservative, Chauncy had saved his tract until circumstances seemed appropriate for its printing. A scholarly treatise on the nature of the episcopal office in patristic thought from the time of Barnabas to that of Clement of Alexandria, it demonstrated that he was one of the foremost colonial authorities on the Fathers.[35]

In examining the writings of the Fathers as collected in

Archbishop Wake's edition, Chauncy sought definitive word regarding the office of bishop, for, Chauncy noted, advocates of episcopacy and the doctrine of apostolic succession frequently claimed support for their position in the writings of the Fathers and argued that an episcopal form of ecclesiastical government replicated the administration of the early church. If the Fathers spoke of bishops as possessing unique authority in church governance, ordination, and confirmation, then the Anglican case would be proved. But if bishops in the earliest church did not have such responsibilities, then the Congregationalist case for equating bishops and presbyters would rest on solid ground.

Chauncy noted, for example, that the Epistle of Barnabas never referred to bishops at all, nor did the writings attributed to Dionysius the Aeropagite, whose authenticity Chauncy duly recognized as questionable. With the *Shepherd of Hermas,* the situation became more complex. The work clearly mentioned bishops, but Chauncy argued, probably correctly in the light of later scholarship, that the bishops described in the *Shepherd* were not persons of superior rank, but men of equal rank whose realm of authority was limited to their specific congregations. Chauncy was careful to treat passages where his interpretation was open to challenge. The *Shepherd* referred to those who envied the "first chair." Did the mere mention of a first chair imply superiority in rank? Not so, at least in Chauncy's mind. The *Shepherd*'s concern should be seen merely as a warning against all pride and envy.

With Clement of Rome, Chauncy again dealt with passages which lie open to variant interpretation. Those who proclaimed the doctrine of apostolic succession frequently called upon Clement of Rome to bolster their position since Clement, as bishop of Rome, could be construed as the successor to St. Peter. Chauncy deftly played historian and textual critic, rehearsing the ambiguities surrounding Clement's tenure as bishop and the numerous problems involved in determining which of the writings attributed to Clement could accurately be traced to his hand. Chauncy noted that those works, such as the Apostolical Constitutions, the Apostolic Canons, and the Recognitions, which advanced a high concept of bishops and episcopal authority were all of questionable authorship and should not even be assigned to the apostolic age. The circumstances reflected in these works, Chauncy argued, belonged to the late second or early third century. Hence, they could not be used to support either the historical primacy of episcopal government in the church or the doctrine of apostolic succession.

In interpreting the genuine work of Clement, the First Letter to the Church at Corinth, Chauncy used Clement's salutation in the name of the Church at Rome to suggest that Clement did not view his own office as granting him authority over others. He wrote simply in the name of the congregation to which he was pastor, calling for consistency in church government among the various Christian communities. By episcopacy, Chauncy concluded, Clement meant only pastoral oversight of a flock, not the primacy of one person over many churches. Hence, for Clement, bishops and presbyters were synonymous titles. With satisfaction, Chauncy recalled that Clement was remembered as a "constant laborer, preacher of the Word, and dispenser of gospel ordinances" as any ordinary pastor, but not as an eighteenth century Anglican bishop would be regarded.[36]

Chauncy continued his journey through the literature of the Apostolic Fathers, gathering more ammunition for his cause. Irenaeus referred to Polycarp of Smyrna as both bishop and presbyter, Chauncy smugly noted, and Polycarp himself seemed to have recognized only two orders, presbyters and deacons, rather than three. The numerous epistles ascribed to Ignatius, who was not mentioned by either Irenaeus or Clement of Alexandria, presented so many textual problems that it was difficult, thought a skeptical Chauncy, to build any argument from them. But Chauncy could not deny that these documents used bishop and presbyter to denote two different offices. Chauncy did stress, however, that the language used was part of the problem of the texts and seemed to require assigning the literature to a much later age. And even if one were to accept the corpus as authentic, one still did not find mention of bishops whose office resembled that of the Church of England bishops. Bishops seemed to be simply officers of local congregations, sharing responsibility with presbyters and deacons, without any spiritual superiority. Any precedence granted to these bishops came from their heading the administration of a single Christian society, not from their having extraordinary powers. Chauncy was adamant in insisting that in no way could the bishops discussed in the Ignatian corpus be construed as diocesan bishops. The diocesan episcopacy, in which a bishop had authority over several congregations, remained an invention of humankind in Chauncy's mind.

And so the cataloguing of comments on the episcopal office continued, through the work of Papias, Quadratus, Justin Martyr, Clement of Alexandria, and numerous others. Nowhere could Chauncy find a portrait of bishops who at all resembled the bishops he found in the Church of England. Wherever bishops were mentioned, they were preachers and pastors diligently ministering to particular congregations. Never were bishops administrators over dioceses, agents of government, or a superior order of clergy. And nowhere could Chauncy find a clear case for affirming the idea of apostolic succession. Indeed, if there were no bishops who exercised superior authority, there could be no apostolic succession to transmit that authority.

What Chauncy did not see, of course, was that the presbyters or elders mentioned in apostolic literature may likewise have borne no resemblance to the elders of his beloved New England Congregationalism. He remained blind to the possibility that the role of elders could have changed over the centuries, just as the role of bishops could have changed. The former he could not acknowledge, for it would have undercut the polity which gave coherence to the New England Way.

The other he refused to acknowledge because to do so would have required accepting episcopal church government as legitimate. At all costs, the New England way must remain the only legitimate replication of the structure of the early church. On the controversial issues concerning the potential political powers of colonial bishops, the possibility of taxation for their support, and the formal establishment of the Church of England in all the colonies, Chauncy said nothing, probably because the manuscript had been completed years before those concerns were the religious talk of the day.

While the controversy was raging, Chauncy had sought to mobilize his fellow dissenting clergymen on both sides of the Atlantic for a carefully organized attack. He proposed a general meeting of concerned American clergy and expanded the scope of his correspondence with English dissenters.[37] Although he received modest assurances of support from a group of London dissenters, he ultimately abandoned the idea of a trans-Atlantic remonstrance because he felt it would only incense advocates of the plan even more. He also found that English support for joint protest diminished when Anglicans claimed that an American bishop would have only spiritual authority.[38] His efforts to unify American clergy were likewise destined to failure, although he did receive some encouragement when the Congregational clergy of Connecticut at their annual meeting in 1768 voted to thank him "for the good service he had done to the cause of religious liberty and truth, in his judicious answer to the Appeal for an American episcopate and in his defense of the New England church and colonies against the unjust reflections cast upon them in the bishop of Landaff's sermon."[39] Others did not think Chauncy's efforts deserving of praise. The New York press, pro-Anglican in tone, simply denounced him as a liar.[40]

In the exchange with Chandler, Chauncy had opposed what he considered to be a threat to both the religious and political liberties of New England. The content of those liberties was essentially the same as the content of the liberty he had defended against the evangelical onslaught during the Awakening. He knew the history of Anglican oppression against the dissenters in England in the seventeenth century; he and most of his fellow New Englanders were of dissenting stock. To structure a church and to worship according to traditional Puritan precepts comprised the core of what he sought to protect. As Alan Heimert correctly asserted, Chauncy and his "liberal" confreres did not engage in this controversy in order to incite the multitude, but to convince the reasonably intelligent who might otherwise tolerate episcopacy that the establishment of an American bishopric would shatter their liberties.[41]

The doctrinal arguments Chauncy presented and his catalogue-like listing of patristic views on episcopacy did not deny the validity of the episcopal office as much as they affirmed that the scriptural duties of bishops were already exercised in New England by ordinary ministers (presbyters). The presence of Church of England bishops who would try to usurp an already functioning office would destroy the foundations of the New England Way. If any religious orientation had domination in influencing the political sector, Chauncy wanted it to be his brand of New England Congregationalism, not an established Church of England. Chauncy neither acknowledged nor denied the *de facto* political clout of Congregationalism in New England, but he would never give another church *de jure* power.

By 1771 when Chauncy's scholarly work appeared, the immediacy of the threat of episcopacy had begun to recede. Even Chauncy had come to believe that the proposal was less odious than he had at first presumed. On June 14, 1771, he wrote to Ezra Stiles: "The establishment of an episcopate may be greatly hurtful; but I firmly believe we shall outlive, and outgrow any inconvenience arising therefrom."[42] However, he also admitted that he would never retreat publicly from his earlier position.[43] Other concerns, particularly political problems in America's colonial relationship with Britain, had eclipsed the dangers of bishops in the public mind, though the controversy had increased colonial discontent with British rule. As John Adams was to recall in 1818 when commenting on the causes of the split with Britain:

> If any gentleman suppose this controversy to be nothing to the present purpose, he is grossly mistaken. It spread universal alarm against the authority of Parliament. It excited a general and just apprehension that bishops, and dioceses, and churches, and priests, and tithes, were to be imposed on us by Parliament. It was known that neither king, nor ministry, nor archbishops, could appoint bishops in America, without an act of Parliament; and if Parliament could tax us, they could establish the Church of England, with all its creeds, articles, tests, ceremonies, and tithes, and prohibit all other churches, as conventicles and schism shops.[44]

But possible bishops were not the only ghosts to haunt Chauncy during this period. Two episodes in the 1760s revived the spectre of Awakening enthusiasm in Chauncy's mind. The first stemmed from the arrival in the fall of 1764 of the Scottish preacher Robert Sandeman. In Scotland, Sandeman had been associated with his father-in-law, John Glas, in spearheading a split in the established Kirk in 1730. Sandeman and Glas had argued that the only way Christians could manifest their faithfulness to the commands of Christ was through the reduplication of the practices and beliefs of the apostolic era. In particular, this restitution of primal Christianity involved strict congregational independency, believers' baptism by immersion, weekly celebration of the Lord's Supper, dependence on a charismatic ministry, the belief that conversion and justification were the immediate and instantaneous work of the Holy Spirit, and literal adherence to scriptural precepts.[45] Privately Chauncy was troubled most by the notion of a charismatic ministry, for he saw all the problems of the evangelical style returning to plague the settled ministry, especially since Sandeman itinerated from place to place.[46]

But his public response focused on Sandeman's understanding of justification and the nature of the Christian life.

In a series of twelve sermons published in one volume, Chauncy amplified the views of salvation and justification—the terms were virtually synonymous for him—which he had begun to articulate during the evangelical revivals.[47] In a logically ordered fashion he traced the development of the Christian doctrine of justification, beginning with its Hebrew antecedents in ancient Israel. His conclusions should not have amazed those who knew him: justification was essentially a process of growth in moral living, the gradual infusion of the Holy Spirit into individual lives, most frequently attained through faithful attendance on the established "means of grace." Indeed, four of the twelve sermons were devoted to a careful examination of the "means of grace" and their importance in bringing human beings within the Christian orbit. Chauncy implicitly dismissed Sandeman's rigid emphasis on strict obedience to biblical injunctions as a form of legalism superseded by the "means of grace." But he did not deny that a close relationship existed between faith and conduct such as Sandeman found outlined in scriptural precepts.

Chauncy drew on the long-standing Puritan tenet that one's works always mirrored the state of one's soul to claim that genuine faith always involved a change in habits and conduct, but he did suggest that ordinarily such change was gradual and transpired as an individual rationally and earnestly sought to develop a Christian character. Mildly Arminian in tone, Chauncy's treatises sought to bring together the three components which he saw as integral to salvation: divine grace, human effort, and the "means of grace" which enabled human effort to appropriate divine grace and thus achieve both salvation and justification. As he noted in the concluding sermon, "The plain truth is, God, man, and means are all concerned in the formation of that character, without which we cannot inherit eternal life."[48]

Although Sandeman's preaching caused some stir among

New England evangelicals, his direct impact was minimal and short lived. His views on the restoration of early Christian practice, however, were to have significant influence on Alexander Campbell, the founder of what became the Disciples of Christ, who spent much time with a group of Sandeman's followers while he was studying in Edinburgh.

Destined to have a more direct effect on the shape of New England religious life was the other movement in which Chauncy saw a possible rebirth of the evangelical spirit. By the late 1760s several sermons and tracts authored by John Murray, a British convert to Methodism who had become a devotee of the Universalist preacher James Relly, were receiving a wide reading in New England. Murray himself emigrated to America in 1770, settling in Massachusetts in 1772 and organizing the first Universalist church in the United States in 1779. When Murray arrived, Chauncy was already developing opinions in "the pudding" (a code name for his last major work), which were closely akin to Relly's and Murray's belief that the work of Christ was designed to secure salvation not just for the elect but for the whole of humanity. But he was especially apprehensive of both the way in which Murray articulated his position and of the style in which he reportedly sought to convince others of the validity of his views.

Murray possessed an oratorical power akin to Whitefield's and by sheer force of personality gained many converts to Universalism. But to Chauncy, Murray's manner reeked of the old evangelicalism, and he would have nothing to do with the man regardless of possible private sympathy with his theological views. Accordingly, when concerned Boston clergy placed a statement in the Boston *News-Letter* highly critical of Murray, Chauncy added his name to the list of those who endorsed it.[49] But it is likely that Chauncy supported the attack on Murray because of the latter's presumed evangelical style rather than because of the seemingly unorthodox theological position which aroused the consternation of his associates.[50]

Meanwhile Chauncy continued to execute the numerous

extra-parish duties which presented themselves. On April 30, 1766, he preached the sermon when Samuel Checkley's assistant was installed and offered the closing prayer on November 19 at the ordination of Samuel Blair as associate of his uncle, Joseph Sewall, at Old South.[51] That same year he was called on to preach the funeral discourse for his close friend and ally Jonathan Mayhew and several months later received the honor of delivering the sermon when Simeon Howard was ordained as Mayhew's successor at the West Church.[52] Chauncy also served as requested on ecclesiastical councils and committees, sharing in the deliberations which acquitted but censured the Reverend Penuel Bowen for possible plagiarism, and meeting with members of Old South as they discussed a course of action in 1769 after Sewall's death and Blair's subsequent resignation.[53] Chauncy had already had the unpleasant duty of preaching Sewall's funeral sermon in July of that year, a few weeks after he had delivered the funeral discourse for his senior associate at Old Brick, Thomas Foxcroft.[54] Boston looked to Chauncy for ministerial service in 1766 when he again opened the town meeting with prayer and in 1768 when he was appointed first to a town committee to report on conditions in the city's almshouses and then to a committee, which also numbered James Otis, John Hancock, and Samuel Adams among its members, to inspect Rainsford Island.[55]

But pastoral duty, ecclesiastical controversy, and potential evangelical threats quickly took a back seat to political concerns. The repeal of the Stamp Act may have been a cause for rejoicing, plans for a bishopric successfully thwarted, and the work of men such as Sandeman and Murray contained and countered. But the jubilation was momentary. Relations between the American colonies and their mother country were deteriorating instead of improving, and soon Chauncy found himself transformed from Puritan pastor to patriot preacher.

5.

Seasonable Revolutionary

The Stamp Act may have generated the most demonstrative protest the colonies raised against British policies in the 1760s, but it was far from the only source of political discontent. Even before Parliament had enacted and rescinded the hated tax, Americans were grumbling over changes in British colonial operations. In 1761, conflict developed over the phenomenon of "Writs of Assistance." Designed to facilitate enforcement of customs regulations, the Writs enabled crown officials to enter privately owned homes, warehouses, ships, and the like without obtaining search warrants in order to ferret out smuggled or illegally imported goods.[1] James Otis championed the colonial cause, arguing that the Writs were themselves illegal and violated the sanctity of private property so highly valued in Puritan New England.[2] The question of legality or illegality aside, the Writs were popularly regarded as an infringement on the rights of the people grounded in the authority of a Parliament in which the colonists had no direct representation and to which they had not delegated power to frame such legislation.

Another focus of discontent centered on the structure of the colonial judiciary. In England judges held life tenure and were therefore regarded as not likely to yield to pressure from persons or institutions seeking to promote their own special interests. Judges in the colonies, however, served at the pleasure of the governor and were considered somewhat less independent than their English counterparts. General objection to the colonial system, based on the belief that an independent judiciary more effectively safeguarded liberty because judges would be less prone to submit to outside influence, was widespread in the 1760s.[3]

Specific questions about control of the judiciary came to the fore in 1767 with the creation of four vice-admiralty courts in the North American colonies. These courts were completely independent of indigenous colonial political structures and, therefore, seemed to interfere with colonial administration of justice. Concern intensified in 1768 when the vice-admiralty courts discarded trial by jury as an inefficient process.[4] The colonists regarded the latter move as especially destructive of the proper ends of government, because determination of innocence, guilt, or punishment rested with a single individual who could easily promote personal advantage at the expense of the general welfare. This policy change appeared not only to negate the right of individuals to receive judgment from a group of their peers, but to deny one rationale for the existence of government, the avoidance of arbitrary rule.[5] In the ensuing turmoil, combatants on both sides forgot that the vice-admiralty courts were intended simply to deal with violations of imperial trade regulations.

Another dimension of the judiciary problem concerned the salaries of government officials. Even though local judges were appointed by the governors, their salaries were determined by the colonial legislatures. Through control of the purse, the elected representatives of the people thought they maintained some check on the power exercised by judges. Judges of the vice-admiralty courts, as officers of the crown, received their salaries directly from the royal treasury. To the colonial mind, this arrangement spelled disaster. Not only had the establishment of the vice-admiralty courts demolished the colonists' right to trial by jury, it had destroyed whatever control they might have been able to exert over the judges as well, since they had no power to pay or withhold salaries. The announcement made in the summer of 1772 that all crown officials in the colonies, from the governors on down, would be paid from the royal exchequer sparked increased distress, for now all branches of colonial government, save the legislative, would be completely outside the control of the people or their elected representatives.[6] The possibility of paying royal governors from crown funds had been frequently raised in earlier days, but an attempt in 1728 to make the Massachusetts governor a crown-paid official had aroused such hostility that the matter had been dropped. Now with no check on government officials remaining, New Englanders felt they had lost their liberties and were doomed to political slavery.[7]

While the colonial legislatures had lost whatever control that power of the purse had provided, the colonists themselves continued indirectly to bear the financial burden of paying government salaries. In 1767 Parliament passed a sequel to the Stamp Act in the form of a series of bills known collectively as the Townshend Acts. To avoid some of the objections to the Stamp Act, the new legislation provided for more extensive import duties in an effort to construe the levies as taxes which Parliament, as the ultimate overseer of trade and commerce in the empire, could legitimately raise. But the purpose of the Townshend duties was evident from the start: they would gain revenue to pay the crown-appointed administrators and bureaucrats serving in the colonies. Once again colonial protest mobilized. While some accepted the legality of the Townshend Acts as devices to regulate colonial commerce, others regarded the laws as destructive of colonial liberty because the products taxed—paint, lead, paper, tea—were among those which the colonists were obliged to purchase through England alone. Since Americans could not turn elsewhere to secure these goods, they could not avoid paying the taxes on them.

When it appeared that the reasoned protest which had brought repeal of the Stamp Act would not produce the same result with the Townshend Acts, the colonists decided to try another strategy: a boycott of all nonessential goods which could be obtained only from England. While the boycott quickly cut into the prosperity of the colonial mercantile business and ultimately made smuggling a way of life for many, it was also intended to have sufficiently deleterious effects on the business of British merchants who could more effectively pressure Parliament to withdraw the measures. Chauncy saw the devious connection between the Townshend duties and the loss of colonial financial control over government officials. He endorsed the boycott at the risk of losing some support among the merchant families in his congregation. Writing to Richard Price some four years after the boycott had been in operation, he commented that "our Governor and the Judges of our highest executive Court are made wholly independent of the people here, and so dependent on administration at home that we can expect no other conduct in them but what will be pleasing to those who are endeavoring to foster on us the chains of slavery. . . ."[8]

In Boston the issue which served to mobilize even greater resentment of Parliamentary policy was the continuing presence of British troops in the city. After the close of the wars with France, Parliament had not recalled all British soldiers to the mother country, but stationed several regiments in the colonies, ostensibly to provide ongoing defensive protection of America. Actually a multitude of secondary factors played into the decision to leave troops in America, ranging from a desire to increase royal military patronage to the need to maintain an upper hand in the peace negotiations with France. At the same time, policy makers had to contend with a British public outraged at the expenditure of men and money in the struggle.[9] But the English—and on this point the colonists proudly claimed their English heritage—had a deep-seated fear of standing armies.

Because the military operated independently from all civil authority and could therefore develop considerable power especially when not engaged in warfare, standing armies were regarded as potential threats to liberty. Instead the English traditionally operated during peacetime with volunteer militias. Men drawn from the ranks of the citizenry were less likely to endanger the welfare of the people by seeking power than was a standing army, it was thought, since the interests of militia members were identical to those of the people. Many also suspected that the soldiers were really on hand to enforce Parliamentary legislation which the colonists regarded as inimical to their well-being and would simply tighten the noose Parliament was slipping around their collective neck. The troops readily became a visible symbol of presumed oppression. Boston's town meeting finally declared officially that the presence of a standing army was an infringement on the rights of the people, a point Chauncy had made privately in a letter to Ezra Stiles in 1768.[10]

A related problem was the matter of underwriting the expenses of supporting a standing army. John Dickinson declared that if Parliament could require the colonists to accept the presence of a standing army it could likewise require payment of new taxes for its support.[11] Such taxes would have to be legislated without the consent of the people, for none believed them—or the army—to be necessary. Parliament had already attempted to deal with this potential tinderbox in the Quartering Act of 1765 which required the provinces to provide barracks and specified supplies for the soldiers, but left to the individual colonial legislatures determination of means to secure the necessary funds. While the colonists were slow to protest this supposed intrusion on their prerogatives, when they did Parliament responded by suspending uncooperative legislatures, including the Massachusetts General Court.

Months of protest against the presence of British soldiers in Boston climaxed March 5, 1770, in the celebrated Boston Massacre. When Dr. Chauncy first learned of the incident, he became furious. Tory Peter Oliver, recording Chauncy's reported remarks concerning Captain Preston, who had commanded the British Regulars involved in the affair, added his own commentary:

> "If I was to be one of the Jury upon his Trial, I would bring him in guilty; *evidence or no Evidence.*" What a noble instance of Divinity, Zeal, Rancor & Revenge, jumbled together into one Mass. But he [Chauncy] had imbibed more of the Temper of *James* & *Peter,* than that of his & their Master. He was always calling down Fire from Heaven to destroy his political opposers.[12]

On May 30 following the "violence," Chauncy preached to a "crowded assembly" after which he and selected other ministers dined at Faneuil Hall as guests of several of the town merchants and "other Sons of Liberty."[13] The sermon soon appeared in print. Using the jeremiad form, Chauncy called upon his listeners to trust in God for deliverance from the present assault on political liberty symbolized by the quartering of British military forces in Boston. He likewise bemoaned the taxation and commercial difficulties which the colonists suffered at the hands of the mother country because of increasingly oppressive mercantile legislation passed by Parliament. Why had Parliament demolished colonial liberty and how could it be regained? The sins of the people were obviously the primary cause of the present turmoil—even the policies of the British government were only a secondary means to convey the wrath of God—and loss of political liberty was a deserved punishment for sin. If citizens wanted their liberty restored, declared Chauncy, they should imitate their Puritan forefathers' virtues: trust in God, repentance, and amendment of life. Once the people had atoned for their individual and collective sins, God would again act through the political order to grant his people their rightful liberty.

At the same time, though, Chauncy did not doubt the justice of the colonial position in protesting the actions of the home government. He firmly believed that the Boston Massacre was an abominable assault on human liberty: ". . . the opened earth in one of our streets, in the month of March last, received the streaming blood of many slaughtered, and wounded innocents. So shocking a tragedy was never before acted in this part of the world; and God forbid that it should ever be again."[14]

Clearly, even if the sins of the Bostonians were the ultimate cause of the turmoil, Parliament had overstepped its bounds in keeping an army in Boston which could take constituted authority into its own hands. Parliament thereby shared responsibility for the misery which the city was now forced to endure. Nevertheless, Chauncy closed with a declaration of the unflinching loyalty of the colonists to King George III and asked divine forgiveness for those who portrayed colonists as disloyal because they objected to current policies. Redress of grievances and restoration of the old order, not independence, were the foci of Chauncy's thought at this time.

Celebrations on the anniversary of the Boston massacre each year provided a public platform for expression of increasingly agitated colonial sentiment. In 1772 Chauncy himself preached at the official anniversary service in the Old South Church.[15] Unfortunately, since the sermon was not published, we do not know precisely how he viewed Parliament's continuing "infringement" of colonial political liberties. His reference to "those who are endeavoring to foster on us the chains of slavery" in the letter to Richard Price already quoted would suggest, however, that he was beginning to think that Parliament rather than the colonists' shortcomings should receive primary blame for the ongoing distress. It at least indicates that he was becoming more and more receptive to the popular, if naive, belief that corruption tainted the English government, particularly at the ministerial level, and had sired a grand conspiracy set on demolishing what remnants of liberty the colonists still possessed. There was ample precedent, though perhaps not logic, for this view in the old Puritan notions that "good" rulers would faithfully execute the proper duties of office in advancing the commonwealth, but that "bad" rulers would not.[16]

It was easy to assume that British officials responsible for colonial policy had lost those moral virtues which would have kept them about their rightful duty. It is difficult, if not impossible, to pinpoint evidence of specific incidents of corruption. But it is not difficult to understand that persons came to believe that corruption was rampant. New Englanders had long held that godly rulers would always advocate what the people regarded as enhancing their well-being. Since the British government now acted counter to self-proclaimed colonial interests, its leaders could not be good men, but must be corrupt men. The conviction that corruption dominated English politics therefore acquired the status of truth in a psychological sense, if not in a political sense.[17]

Meanwhile the boycott on English goods had only minimally cut into the prosperity of British merchants who had found new markets for their wares in Asia and elsewhere in Europe. But in 1770, on the same day as the Boston Massacre, Parliament repealed the odious Townshend duties, save for the tax on tea. It was obvious on both sides of the Atlantic that the tea tax had been retained for only one purpose: to assert the legitimacy of Parliamentary authority over the colonies. Hence colonial discontent moved from the specifics of particular policies believed detrimental to American interests to the more abstract yet more fundamental question of whether crown and Parliament held any valid political authority over the colonies. Viewed in this context, the Boston Tea Party of December 1773 did not really represent a protest against the remaining tea tax as much as it signalled a response to that question of authority: all acts of Parliament which the colonists deemed oppressive or regarded as encroaching on their own domain of authority would be resisted.

Parliament returned a challenge with both symbolic and economic ramifications: it closed Boston's port to all trade. If Parliament could enforce this "punishment," its political authority over all aspects of colonial life would be assured. And if the port remained closed for any length of time, the foundations of Boston's merchant economy would crumble, bringing disaster to all New England, for virtually all New England depended on imports channeled through Boston.

Chauncy expressed his personal concern in a letter to Richard Price written May 30, 1774, less than a month after Parliament had declared the port closed:

> The late act of Parliament, shutting up the port of Boston, and putting it out of the power of thousands of poor innocents to preserve themselves from starving, is so palpably cruel, barbarous, and inhumane, that even those who are called friends of Government complain bitterly of it; nor do I know of any whose eyes are not opened to see plainly that despotism, which must end in slavery, is the plan to be carried into execution. This British edict, which, without all doubt, was an intended blow at the liberties of all the American colonies, will, I believe, under the blessing of Providence, be the very thing which will bring salvation to us. The town of Boston, the Massachusetts-Province, and the other Colonies, far from being intimidated by the horrid severity and injustice of this Port-Act, are rather filled with indignation, to render void its designed operation.[18]

Just three days earlier the call had gone forth from Virginia for a continental congress. The tactic of unified protest which had proved effective in combatting the Stamp Act would be attempted again. In Boston a separate town committee delegated Chauncy to draft a report "to be made by this town to Great Britain & all the World" to protest the port closing.[19] In its own way, this open letter reflected Chauncy's personal understanding of the political liberty of the colonies as the right to continue their traditional political and economic practices. In effect, he called for a return to the old order:

> The Bostonians have always been as much disposed to honor and support constitutional government as any of the people of England; and it is one of their greatest burdens that they should be brought into such circumstances, as to be even forced into that which is highly disagreeable to them; and if "the good

> order of Boston" has, in any measure, been disturbed, the way to restore peace is to hear our cries, and redress our grievances. . . . Force may for a while keep the people under restraint; but this very restraint may, in time, be the occasion of the outbreaking of their passions with greater violence; and what the consequence, in that case, will be, God only knows. . . . Even those who have been distinguished by being called friends of government, are now fully satisfied that the plan to be carried into execution, and by forcible measures, is intire [sic] obedience to the demands of despotism, instead of those constitutional laws we are perfectly willing to be governed by. It may reasonably be esteemed an advantage, and a very important one, to be thus indisputably let into the knowledge of this; as by knowing that forcing from us our rights and privileges as English subjects, is the grand point in view, we shall naturally be urged on to contrive expedients to prevent, if possible, our being in this way, brought into bondage.[20]

Chauncy thus finally sanctioned active resistance to British policy because of what he regarded as its despotic intentions. A government which enslaved citizens by destroying their constitutional rights had lost its legal status in his eyes, for Chauncy simply assumed that governments were by definition bound to protect the rights of individuals. "The inhabitants of Boston are English subjects, as well as the citizens of London," he argued, "and may with equal justice utter their cries against that arbitrary exercise of power, which indiscriminately makes use of their rightful property dependant on pleasure at three thousand miles distance. . . ."[21]

Chauncy realized that if the clash between colonial interests and British policy reached an impasse, he would reluctantly endorse the armed conflict which might ensue. "It would be highly grievous," he wrote to Price in July 1774, "and the last thing the Colonies would wish, to be obliged to stand upon their own defense against military force should it be used with them; but this, should no other expedient be effectual, I believe, they would certainly do. All the Colonies desire is the full enjoyment of their rights and priveleges [sic]. . . ."[22] Andrew Eliot put the colonial goals in stronger terms when he commented that independence had quickly become "all everyone discusses now."[23]

In 1774 the Boston clergy signalled their entrance into the camp of those who would resist British policy when, on a motion by Dr. Chauncy, they voted to discontinue the practice of reading formal proclamations issued by the Governor or the Council in their meetinghouses.[24] The economic reprisals of the closing of the Boston port would destroy their mercantile-oriented congregations. The traditional New England way in politics had been threatened, and it was now not only "seasonable," but necessary to resist. The Massachusetts ministers received support from their counterparts in Connecticut. In June 1774 the Congregationalist pastors of that colony sent a letter to Chauncy addressed to the ministers of Boston:

> We consider you as suffering in the common cause of America, in the cause of liberty; which, if taken away, we fear would involve the ruin of religious liberty also. . . . [We] commend your cause, and the cause of America, the cause of liberty, and, above all, the cause of religion, to the Father of mercies, who can easily offer effectual relief. . . ."[25]

When the Continental Congress convened in Philadelphia on September 5, 1774, Chauncy avidly followed its deliberations and sought to make sure that the plight of Boston was impressed on the minds of the delegates from the eleven other colonies which sent representatives. When Josiah Quincy, Jr., arrived in Philadelphia to plead Boston's cause, he carried with him letters of introduction from Chauncy to numerous Massachusetts delegates requesting that they in turn present him to those in power so he could seek their assistance which was urgently needed as "we groan under the oppressive burdens y^t lie heavy on us."[26] But in the letter introducing Quincy to Samuel Adams, Chauncy noted that Bostonians remained in good spirits, although he feared that the Coercive

Acts which closed Boston's port would "hasten what I hope could be deferred and forever unless necessary"—military resistance and open rebellion.[27] For a time Chauncy sensed that the stern nonimportation, nonexportation, and nonconsumption resolutions adopted by the Congress would induce Britain to relent, but as Boston became "surrounded by land and sea by those who would destroy us," he realized that a bloody contest loomed ahead as citizens hardened in their determination to defend themselves against tyranny.[28]

Chauncy's reluctant, but relentless, advocacy of the patriot cause quickly became well known on both sides of the Atlantic. In September 1774 a handbill listing the names of the fifteen most dangerous men in Boston passed among the British troops in the area. While the circular may have been a propaganda piece issued by colonial patriots to arouse popular indignation when individuals realized that the town's most prominent citizens were regarded as criminals, the inclusion of Chauncy's name on the list indicates that he was perceived by local rebels as an active supporter of the independence movement.[29] And when one-time Massachusetts Governor Thomas Hutchinson mentioned Chauncy by name to His Majesty the King, George III replied that he had heard much about the patriot preacher's activities.[30] Chauncy wasted little compassion on Hutchinson. When it was suggested that Hutchinson, as a Massachusetts native, might be able to use his position as governor to extricate the colony from its predicament, Chauncy reportedly declared that he would "rather the Country should perish than be saved by him."[31] Chauncy simply could not comprehend how a native son, even though now a crown-appointed official, could execute royal policies so bitterly opposed by his life-long friends. Nor could Chauncy envision the anguish that Hutchinson faced when forced by his position, if not by his inclination, to choose between British demands and the wishes of his fellow Massachusetts subjects. Few patriots then, and few historians since, have given Hutchinson his due.[32]

From April to July of 1774, with British troops hovering on all sides of the city, Chauncy felt it necessary to retreat to Medfield, some twenty miles away, for his own safety, and when the British took full control of Boston in May 1775 after military hostilities had begun, Chauncy again fled the city and remained in exile until after American forces entered the town in 1776. Although advancing in years and frequently in ill health, Chauncy maintained a lively interest in the progress of the American cause. Massachusetts honored his unswerving support in 1775 by naming him to a commission charged with designing a new official seal for the commonwealth.[33] No doubt he also took pride in the political activity of his son and sons-in-law.[34] His son, for example, served on the Kittery Committee of Safety and as a delegate to New Hampshire's first provincial congress in 1774, and twice he was elected to the New Hampshire Revolutionary Council (1776, 1777), but declined the honor.

When word reached Boston that the Continental Congress had adopted the Declaration of Independence, the elderly pastor at Old Brick rejoiced. Abigail Adams wrote to her husband, John, describing the service at First Church that August Sunday in 1776 when Chauncy read the Declaration to those assembled for worship:

> . . . The Dr. concluded with asking a blessing "upon the United States of America even until the final restitution of all Things." Dr. Chauncy's address pleased me. The good man after having read it lifted his eyes and hands to heaven. "God bless the United States of America, and let all the people say Amen." One of his audience told me it universally struck them.[35]

But the good doctor harbored some private reservations about the depth of commitment to resistance among many of his fellow Boston aristocrats. He may stand guilty of molding a theology palatable to the mercantile class and of usually equating the good and happiness of the whole community with the economic good of the merchants, but he did recognize that in order to extricate themselves from their immediate dilemma, merchants might act from motives of self-interest and ignore the larger threat to the liberty of all citizens which their peculiar plight epitomized. He had expressed his doubts when he first wrote to Price about the closing of the port:

> . . . We have found by experience, that no dependence can be had upon *merchants,* either at *home,* or in *America.* So many of them are so mercenary as to find within themselves a readiness to become slaves themselves, as well as be accessory to the slavery of others, if they imagine they may, by this means, serve their own private interest. Our dependence, under God, is upon the *landed interest,* upon freeholders and yeamonry [sic].[36]

Chauncy's skepticism did not mean that he had suddenly shifted his loyalties from the mercantile to the agrarian. Heimert correctly interpreted this passage as an indication of Chauncy's heartfelt commitment to the established New England social order, persons of many classes and occupations, freeholders and yeomen included, with the Boston mercantile aristocracy in its rightly earned place of special prominence.[37] But a threat to one class was in the last analysis a threat to all. Redress of grievances, therefore, must be sought for all through appropriate channels. If the merchants acted strictly on their own behalf, they would have failed to exercise the duties and obligations incumbent upon them because of their superior station in a hierarchically ordered society.

The disruptions brought by the conflict intruded into every area of social life. Printers, for example, offered a decidedly more political fare and less of the traditional materials, including sermons. Chauncy himself published only one sermon during the years of the War for Independence. Again adopting the old form of the jeremiad, he noted that sin was too often "in the midst of a people when engaged in war."[38] People on both sides in a war may have sinned, Chauncy declared, but unless those whose cause was just removed sin from their midst, it was impossible to determine to whom God would finally grant victory.[39] Chauncy singled out the one specific sin which he believed most hindered the otherwise just cause of New England. It was a sin against which he had inveighed some thirty years earlier in his inflammatory election sermon: New Englanders had an insatiable thirst for money, reflected in a paper currency situation destined, as always, to keep clergymen's salaries at an abominably low level in terms of real value.[40] The political order had a moral obligation to provide for those powerless to alter their own financial status—widows, orphans, and ministers. Even in war, such persons should not be made to suffer because others had made themselves rich. General repentance and reformation were once again needed if Americans were to receive God's blessing and, more to the point, regain their cherished liberties.

Again Chauncy had linked political liberty and economic liberty. The responsibility of the political realm to promote "commercial stability and an efficient economy" in society included securing the right of Boston merchants to engage in trade without unnecessary interference from across the Atlantic so that these same merchants could exercise their proper role in the New England social hierarchy by caring for the needs of those who had no economic power. Chauncy naively believed that the requisite stability for an efficient economy had prevailed before the 1760s, but that the passage of the Stamp Act and subsequent Parliamentary actions culminating in the closing of Boston's port had decisively altered the situation. Stability and efficiency would return, he thought, if the old order were defended and restored. But preservation of the old order now demanded active resistance and rebellion.[41]

But why did Chauncy come to regard Revolutionary activity as the best means to preserve colonial liberty? Quite simply, Chauncy was concerned with the transmission of those social and political patterns which he perceived as integral to a developing American identity and self-awareness, patterns which included a prosperous mercantile economy, the relative independence of colonial legislatures (especially in matters of taxation), the tacit hegemony of the fragmented Puritan establishment in New England religious life, recognition of American military ability, and the withdrawal of British troops from Boston. In short, Chauncy looked to the pre-1763 social order as representing a complex structure which had allowed a haphazardly defined political and religious liberty to flourish. He did not consider whether his perception of the past was factually accurate or whether the structures he wanted to preserve could be defended on legal grounds. In other words, Chauncy was concerned less with the formalities and technicalities of a colonial relationship with Great Britain than he was with what he and his fellow Americans had come to accept as a viable and legitimate way of ordering their common life.[42]

In the debate over the power to tax, control over the salaries of government officials, and the right of Parliament to close the Boston port, Chauncy saw disruption of former ways as a threat to the liberty which Americans believed was rightly theirs as English subjects and which they felt they had once enjoyed as members of a social order grounded in civil constitutions and the rule of law. Charles Chauncy did not become involved in activities surrounding colonial independence from Britain because he sought the overthrow of the established political order and hoped to build a new, radically different structure in its place. Rather, he endorsed reasoned resistance and then rebellion in an effort to preserve and protect the forms and institutions of liberty which had evolved in the American context. Chauncy became a patriot in order to restore what he saw as a lost ideal—the ideal of human liberty. He was a Revolutionary because it was "seasonable" to be such.

When the war drew to a close and American victory had been attained—perhaps because Chauncy was correct in his simplistic belief that angels had deflected bullets fired at the

American rebels—the elderly preacher again took up his first love, the study of theology.[43] Released from some of his duties at First Church after 1778 when the congregation had hired John Clarke as his associate, Chauncy returned to his study where he found those manuscripts which he had prepared years before and set aside. Was the time now "seasonable" to offer these, the theological treatises known only to a few close friends, to a people tired of war and political discussion?

6.

The Pudding Is Boiled

While Revolution and politics held top priority for Chauncy in the turbulent decade of the 1770s, he nevertheless found time for those routine clerical functions which had for so long been a part of his life and for continuing work on theological tracts which had been drafted years before. Boston called on him to offer prayer at the annual town meeting in 1770 and again in 1772. In 1777, he was invited to preach the first official Fourth of July anniversary sermon for the city. He willingly performed the first duties, but was forced to decline the last honor for reasons of health.[1] Throughout the war years, he participated whenever possible in ecclesiastical councils, ordinations, and the like.

In 1771, he gave the official charge at the ordination of John Hunt at Old South and in 1773 took part in the installation of Joseph Howe as pastor at New South.[2] In August 1773, he moderated a special council called to protest the dismissal of Thomas Goss from the church at Bolton.[3] His long-standing conviction that dismissals were usually improper and in any case not to be taken lightly is revealed in a caustic remark Chauncy reportedly made to John Walley, who hoped to succeed Goss at Bolton. During the Council's proceedings, Chauncy is said to have turned to the aspiring preacher and muttered, "Walley, do you intend to sit down in this fire? Why, it will burn up your little soul."[4]

That same year he also participated in a council at Dorchester, but fifteen months later when Old South requested him to meet with a council called to adjudicate a congregational dispute, he was so absorbed in political affairs that the church replaced him.[5] In one council, Chauncy's political stance no doubt influenced his clerical judgment. Boston's Hollis Street Church was in the throes of a dispute with its pastor, Mather Byles, in 1777, and Chauncy was tapped to help resolve the problem. Acquaintances noticed a sharp change in Chauncy's attitude from that manifested in earlier councils, for he seemed eager to secure Byles's dismissal. John Eliot claimed that Chauncy angrily dismissed the pastor under investigation by declaring, "Byles is not fit for a preacher."[6] Chauncy urged the proceedings on, supporting the plan to remove Byles from his pulpit because "irregular" times witnessed "irregular" actions.[7] The fact of the matter was that Byles's qualifications and conduct as a pastor were never seriously examined by Chauncy. It was simply a case of Revolutionary politics. Byles was an avowed Tory, and Chauncy the Patriot had as little use for his political opponents as he had for those who questioned his religious stance.

But for Chauncy personally, the theological treatises on which he had labored intermittently for years were more enticing. "Doth he relish the pudding?" Chauncy would excitedly inquire from time to time to learn the opinion of an associate who had perused those manuscripts first drafted in the quiet years after the Awakening.[8] For many years only a select few knew of the existence of "the pudding," and fewer knew that the documents proposed a substantial revision in the doctrine of election by claiming that all persons would ultimately reap the blessings of salvation.

When Chauncy first embarked on his regimen of disciplined theological and scriptural study after the revivals had waned, he recognized that the public could neither appreciate nor accept his developing point of view. Perhaps Chauncy knew that his intentions would be misunderstood.

Many would regard any recasting of the content of doctrine as an attempt to undercut New England theology. Such, of course, was not Chauncy's aim. As always, he was propelled by a conservative passion to preserve the essential structures and categories of Puritan religious thought, but he did want to lend them fresh plausibility in the wake of the rising Enlightenment rationalism which had the potential, unless defused by someone with impeccable Puritan credentials, to destroy the foundations of Puritan belief.[9] To suggest a revamping of any of the theological tenets basic to New England religious life just as the Awakening ebbed could have been to level a death blow to a religious order already fragmented by the evangelical onslaught. It was "seasonable" to wait.

Even when theological controversy erupted in the 1750s over the doctrine of original sin, Chauncy had wisely stayed on the perimeter, witnessing his colleagues becoming absorbed in matters which ordinary folk were willing to bracket for the moment as they tried to pursue their quest for salvation in a divided Congregationalism. So cautious was Chauncy when it came to revealing the results of his inquiry that he declined to allow his friend and ideological ally Jonathan Mayhew to examine the draft, for he believed that Mayhew could not "keep a secret. I am not yet ready or determined to publish [the pudding];" he commented to Ebenezer Gay, "but if [Mayhew] sees [it], such is his frankness that all the world will soon know it."[10] Years later when John Eliot began to read the manuscript he, too, doubted the wisdom of publishing the work. "It will not do to publish it at once, if proper to expose it at all," the pastor of the New North Church wrote in 1779. "It is too sublime for the soaring of vulgar imaginations, & would dazzle, if not blind the eyes of the populace. It would be like the rays of the noon day sun to persons who had never before seen the light."[11] But he hastened to add that more ministers agreed with Chauncy's views than most people would suppose.

Even after John Murray had settled in New England in the 1770s and was gathering adherents to a brand of universalism less palatable to those who sympathized with Chauncy's position, the aging cleric remained reluctant to share his ideas with the world, although friends were encouraging him to do so. The intellectual climate may have been receptive to his writings, but the politics of the Revolution had come to dominate public concern. Eliot, who had become convinced that Chauncy should release his work as an antidote to Murray, noted that Chauncy believed "the present is the worst time which could ever happen, for men's minds are too much absorbed in politics to attend unto anything else."[12] If Chauncy did publish the manuscript, he wanted the time to be "seasonable" for its reception. Eliot also noted that Chauncy feared his more sophisticated and subtle work would be taken by the uninitiated as an endorsement of Murray's universalism or, worse still, utilized by Murray to strengthen his own case. Of course, Chauncy could have added criticisms of Murray's theological views to his own manuscript, but he chose to let the opportunity pass. Perhaps he fully realized that he basically agreed with Murray's thinking. But Chauncy could never accept what seemed to him to be a lack of respect for traditional New England church order on Murray's part.

Yet soon Murray would have to be answered, and soon there would have to be a response to the new attacks on orthodox theology which came from the pens of Revolutionary heroes such as Ethan Allen and Tom Paine. Infidelity could also make serious dents in the precarious structure of New England theology unless defenders of the faith stepped forward. Besides, by the early 1780s so many persons had sampled "the pudding" that it was becoming increasingly difficult to keep its existence a secret. Even Chauncy was less restrained in his caution. At an ecclesiastical council in January 1782, called to examine Oliver Everett, candidate for ordination and installation at New South, Chauncy lost his temper when some of the laymen present questioned Everett's orthodoxy.

Chauncy, of course, believed that the laymen should simply follow the lead of the clergy who were, after all, the theological professionals. In addition, he no doubt privately agreed with many of Everett's views. Accordingly, when the lay delegates challenged Everett's interpretation of the doctrine of the Trinity, "Dr. Chauncy grew mad, told Deacon Jeffres he was a fool, & Deacon Greenough that he knew nothing, & was fit only to lift up his hand, which was all any body expected from him. . . . It was lucky the dispute turned upon the article of the trinity & exhausted the patience of the Council, for this was only a prelude to other matters which would have set us all aghast," recounted John Eliot. "We might have been obliged to eat the pudding, bag & all."[13]

But at last "the pudding" was served. With John Clarke, the younger associate at Old Brick, Chauncy first prepared a document which was little more than a collection of what other writers had already said on universal salvation. Chauncy dashed off a brief preface, attacking Murray's stance as such "an *encouragement* to *Libertinism*" that many had "lost all sense of religion," and the pamphlet finally appeared in August 1782 over the signature of "One Who Wishes Well to All Mankind."[14] The anticipated furor materialized. While John Eliot knew that the piece was but "a meer castrated edition of the whole work," he bemoaned the controversy which was brewing. On September 30, 1782 he wrote to Jeremy Belknap:

> We are here all in a flame re[garding] the controversy concerning the duration of future punishment. Dr. Chauncy & Clarke have let the cat out of ye bag. They begun by printing a sermon, or rather essay, containing the opinions of others upon this subject, which by no means served their cause, for it is not well done. Clarke then opened the subject in the pulpit, & in conversation with his people, and it hath given universal disgust.[15]

Unfortunately, Eliot noted, only the Murrayites liked it. Murray himself, however, gave only qualified approval:

> As for this anonymous advocate . . . I pity him from my soul; I see he is endeavoring, by seasoning the gospel with a sufficient quantity of fire and brimstone, to render quite a savory dish for the self-righteous pharisee. . . . Yet, in this small pamphlet there are a great many good things. I think the author meant well.[16]

The more orthodox leaped at the opportunity to attack the aging foe of evangelicalism. Several rejoinders appeared at once. Jonathan Edwards the younger, Samuel Mather, Peter Thacher, Samuel Hopkins, and William Gordon all offered tracts to counter Chauncy, but only one, *Divine Glory Brought to View in the Condemnation of the Ungodly* authored by Princeton graduate Joseph Eckley, triggered an immediate reply from Chauncy while the work was in press in London.[17] Chauncy's retort, with its title *Divine Glory Brought to View in the Final Salvation of All Men* (1783) a play on Eckley's, set forth his views more boldly.

In 1784 Chauncy published the two most significant works in his universalist corpus: *The Benevolence of the Deity* which provided the theological framework for the whole scheme, and "the pudding" which arrived from England bearing the title *The Mystery Hid from Ages and Generations Made Manifest by the Gospel-Revelation.* The following year, he issued his last major work, *Five Dissertations on the Scriptural Account of the Fall.* Together, the five treatises left an indelible mark on the New England theological landscape, providing an embryonic ideology for advocates of Unitarianism in the nineteenth century. Yet it is unlikely that Chauncy believed he was shattering the foundations of traditional religious belief. Rather, as was so often the case throughout his life, Chauncy was no doubt convinced that he was simply offering a "seasonable," logical explication of scriptural truth.

The pivotal notion which tied together the theological doctrines dissected in these works was Chauncy's idea of the benevolence of God. To ascribe benevolence to the Deity was certainly within the bounds of orthodox statement. Although other heirs of Puritanism might have labelled "sovereignty" the foremost divine attribute, none would deny that the Creator was benevolent, especially in offering to the elect a means of eternal happiness which as sinners they did not deserve. But Chauncy was never one to refuse to push an idea to its logical rational extreme. Accordingly, he argued that a truly benevolent God would not have brought anything into existence without concomitantly both willing and possessing the power to effect its final and complete happiness. It then stood to reason that as moral and rational creations of a benevolent Deity, all persons must ultimately be destined to everlasting happiness, the fruit of salvation.

> As the First Cause of all things is infinitely benevolent, 'tis not easy to conceive, that he should bring mankind into existence, unless he intends to make them finally happy. And if this was his intention, it cannot well be supposed, as he is infinitely intelligent and wise, that he should be unable to project, to carry into execution, a scheme that would be effectual to secure, sooner or later, the certain accomplishment of it.[18]

For Chauncy benevolence was intimately linked to the glory of God. Any pious New Englander knew that promotion of the divine glory was God's primary business and assumed that, in the words of the Westminster Shorter Catechism, "man's chief end is to glorify God and to enjoy him forever." But Chauncy had deflected the thrust of that affirmation by equating human happiness with the glory of God. In his scheme God reaped the greatest glory in those expressions of benevolence which promoted creaturely happiness. As Joseph Haroutunian has noted, "Before the good of man consisted ultimately in glorifying God; now the glory of God consists in the good of man. Before man lived to worship and to serve God, and now God lives to serve human happiness."[19] Another way to put it is to say that Chauncy had shifted the cornerstone of religious thought from a theocentric anthropology to an anthropocentric theology. But at the same time he had not discarded the theological categories—sin, the work of Christ, salvation, and the like—associated with orthodoxy. He simply began from a different starting point, rearranged and reformulated doctrinal explication, and arrived at an unorthodox destination.

Chauncy turned to a form of natural theology as well as to Scripture to demonstrate the primacy of divine benevolence and its connection with human happiness. The created order in its entirety reflected the work of a benevolent God. The interdependence of various inanimate phenomena, for example, revealed an arrangement designed to promote the welfare of all nature. The sun, Chauncy claimed, was in precisely the right location, precisely the appropriate size, and precisely constituted chemically to render the earth a fit habitation for those *"animated,* and *intelligent* beings, who now exist happy on it."[20] Obviously, the world was ordered as it was to advance human happiness.

Chauncy saw the nature of a human being demonstrating divine benevolence even more vividly. The human, as both a physical and spiritual being, shares some qualities with lower animals and some with higher spiritual beings (angels), but acts as a free moral agent. This combination allows humans to enjoy more kinds of happiness than any other creature.[21] Like other animals, humans receive happiness in the satisfaction of physical, sensory needs and desires, but like the angels, they are capable of a higher intellectual and moral happiness.[22] Through rational use of their ability to determine their own actions, humans can actually enhance their own well-being. In Chauncy's mind, the extent of human potential stood as the mark of a benevolent creator.

Chauncy also adopted certain notions from the increasingly popular concept of the Great Chain of Being to bolster his case. As he had argued in the Awakening that the diversity of talents among the clergy brought more glory to God than uniformity, he now expanded the expression of diversity to take in the entire created order. The vastness of creation, with each element in its assigned relationship to each other, surely reflected divine goodness, for the greater the number and type of beings in the world, the greater the glory and benevolence of God could be made manifest.[23] The balance and interconnections proved "the riches and glory of the Creator's goodness, far beyond what it [creation] could have done, if the *continuity* had been broken by the *non-existence* of any of the ranks of creatures, which now make it an *absolutely full and well-connected universe.*"[24] If Chauncy somewhat naively utilized the same concept on occasion to support an aristocratic, hierarchical organization in Boston society, he nevertheless regarded variety and gradation as essential to the structure of any world brought into existence by a benevolent Creator.

But if this world really was the best of all possible ones because of its origins in the divine benevolence, that did not mean the world was necessarily perfect. No Puritan preacher could ever doubt the presence of sin and evil in human life which impeded the attainment of happiness and reminded one and all of the depth of human imperfection and weakness. Hence, despite his conviction that every creature was ultimately destined to enjoy the fullest happiness for which its constitution was designed, Chauncy was more than willing to admit that all persons were not in a state of happiness in this world. Indeed, he acknowledged that apparent flaws in the structure of the universe formed a type of evil which did keep some from complete happiness.[25] But that evil was minimal at best; imperfection, after all, was a necessary corollary to creation since "absolute perfection . . . is an incommunicable glory of the only true God."[26]

The notion of the Great Chain of Being also required that there exist creatures with precisely the abilities and liabilities inherent in human beings and a world with precisely the same flaws as the one humanity inhabited. Chauncy also recognized that what might be called "natural evils" thwarted efforts to achieve happiness.[27] In explanation, as Conrad Wright has noted, Chauncy abandoned his dependence on the Great Chain of Being idea, for he did not argue that those hard facts of life such as pain, labor, and death which comprised the category of "natural evils" were simply incumbent on creatures designed to form a specific link in the Chain.[28] Instead he claimed that the benevolent Deity permitted such evils to exist to fulfill a didactic function. Labor, for example, was requisite to human life in order to provide those increased opportunities for happiness which would come from the use of the earth's resources, but which would be lacking if the earth were left an undeveloped wilderness.[29]

Chauncy identified another type of evil, moral evil or the evil which resulted directly from the actions of human beings.[30] On the one hand, Chauncy claimed that the possibility of moral evil was a logical adjunct both to the free will which the benevolent Creator had given to human beings and to their finite character.[31] As free moral agents, people could act in defiance of their own best interests and hinder attainment of their own happiness as well as that of others. But a world without free moral agents existing in it would of course be one with less variety and would reflect less divine benevolence than one with such creatures. "[T]he making of free agents was *necessary* in order to the communication of the highest good in kind; because, if they had not been made, this kind of good would have been wanting in the creation. . . ."[32]

More significant to Chauncy was the reverse possibility: if humans were capable of moral evil, they were likewise capable of moral good.[33] And that latter capacity was the prelude to happiness. To be sure, sin and evil were so prevalent that persons could not exercise their inherent capacity and desire for the good without divine assistance, but they were not helpless. They simply needed to be shown that which was good. In this emphasis on human possibility, Chauncy made an important departure from orthodoxy, for he had refrained from calling upon a doctrine of original sin to explain the human predicament and the necessity of divine aid in attaining happiness.

The doubts which Chauncy had guardedly expressed in the debates over original sin twenty-five years earlier had become transformed into a firm denial of the traditional statement of original sin. Now Chauncy regarded the idea of original sin as guilt inherited from Adam as an insult to the moral character of the individual human being which logically made the free individual alone responsible only for personal sin and guilt. At the same time, he felt that no one actually experienced a sense of inherited guilt; hence the notion of original sin was rationally absurd since it demanded belief in that which could not be a part of ordinary experience.[34] One could justifiably be held accountable only for one's own life and conduct. "For sin . . . stands in a necessary connection with the agent who commits it, and must therefore . . . be PERSONAL. One man may be a SUFFERER, in consequence of the sin of another, but one man cannot be *guilty* of another man's sin."[35] The sole sense in which sin could be called "original" was in its being one possibility open to finite creatures, in the free exercise of their wills, who could not attain righteousness without divine help.[36]

But humanity did need a guide who would exemplify that pattern of conduct which would lead away from sin and put one on the path to happiness.[37] In the person and work of Christ, redemption from sin and restoration to a "salvable condition" were potentially offered to all and effectively secured for all who accepted. "The incarnation, obedience, sufferings, and death of Christ are therefore to be considered as the way, or method, in which the wisdom of God thought fit to bring into eventuality the redemption of man."[38] Most frequently referring to Christ as "Son of God," Chauncy placed great emphasis on the mediatorial and exemplary roles of Christ. Christ served as mediator between humanity and divinity because he did not fall into sin, but suffered death in obedience to the divine will, and therefore demonstrated that attainment of ultimate happiness was a real possibility for ordinary human beings. Equally important, Christ served as an example of the life which persons intent on eternal happiness should lead. What was vital to Chauncy's argument here was his belief that Christ was mediator and exemplar not just for the elect, but for all persons. He took one passage in the Book of Romans literally and offered it as scriptural proof for his assertions:

> While we were yet helpless, at the right time Christ died for the ungodly. Why, one will hardly die for a righteous man—though perhaps for a good man one will dare even to die. But God shows his love for us in that while we were yet sinners Christ died for us. Since, therefore, we are now justified by his blood, much more shall we be saved by him from the wrath of God. For if while we were enemies we were reconciled to God by the death of his Son, much more, now that we are reconciled, shall we be saved by his life. Not only so, but we also rejoice in God through our Lord Jesus Christ, through whom we have now received our reconciliation.[39]

Since Christ worked on behalf of all, salvation was open to all. But awareness that one had received salvation did not necessarily come in a single experience of conversion or assurance. The salvific process for Chauncy was primarily an educational enterprise, the gradual development of a style of life in which the will less and less chose that which was sinful and opted more and more for that which Scripture and experience suggested would enhance one's passing into eternal bliss at the last judgment.[40] Both Alan Heimert and James W. Jones have claimed that for Chauncy the attainment of salvation was equivalent to earning a Harvard degree.[41] While their appraisal is too harsh, it does highlight the type of experience which Chauncy saw as fundamental to the Christian life. What did matter to him was that through the agency of the church as guardian of the "means of grace," Christ had provided vehicles which humans could use in their quest for everlasting happiness.

In one sense Chauncy's approach represents a logical outcome of the whole New England apparatus of "preparation for salvation."[42] If one were to devote oneself to attendance on the "means of grace" in the hope of receiving the gift of salvation, did it not stand to reason that the means ought to guarantee what they claimed to provide? Chauncy thought so. After all just as God would not have fashioned any creature without concomitantly willing its attainment of happiness, so God would not have instituted the "means of grace" unless they could accomplish the end for which they were designed.

At the same time Chauncy was articulating a notion which finally made its way into more orthodox circles in the nineteenth century, though not without controversy then, for he was describing salvation as a process of growth in much the same way as Congregationalist Horace Bushnell did in his widely read and hotly debated *Christian Nurture* which appeared in 1847. For both Chauncy and Bushnell, growth or nurture in Christian living replaced the cataclysmic experience of conversion as the normative route to salvation for those born into Christian families. To be sure, Chauncy still believed that the presence of the Spirit in the "means of grace" was a prerequisite to their leading the soul to salvation. But just as he had argued in the Awakening years that the Spirit usually worked in ordinary rather than extraordinary ways, now he viewed ordinary, gradual religious growth and development as the key to final happiness rather than a discrete experience of conversion.

Since evil still existed, it was clear to Chauncy that the world as he knew it was not in a saved state. Individuals, too, despite their good intentions still fell into sin. Chauncy also recognized that logically a righteous God should punish sin and evil because both thwarted the divine desire to bring all creatures to happiness, but he could no longer accept the traditional conclusion that those who were guilty of sin and remained unrepentant would receive as their due punishment eternal damnation in hell.

> It does not appear to me, that it would be honourable to the infinitely righteous and benevolent Governor of the world, to make wicked men *everlastingly miserable.* For, in what point of light soever we take a view of sin, it is certainly in its nature a *finite evil.* It is the fault of a *finite creature,* and the effect of *finite* principles, passions, and appetites. To say, therefore, that the sinner is doomed to *infinite* misery for the *finite* faults of a *finite* life looks like a reflection on the *infinite justice,* as well as goodness, of God.[43]

Whatever punishment the unrepentant received, Chauncy reasoned, should be finite in nature. To strengthen his case, Chauncy revived another of the tenets he had advanced in the Awakening controversy. Then he had argued that the kind of conversion experience one had and the degree of assurance of salvation one received were directly related to personality type and the extent of one's involvement in sin. In the present discussion, he reshaped that point to claim that the nature and duration of punishment would vary according to the sins of the individual concerned, but it would always be finite.[44] Hell for Chauncy thus became an intermediate stage of existence between death on earth and eternal happiness in heaven in which those who had not taken sufficient regard for spiritual nurture would be punished and offered opportunities for religious growth sufficient to guarantee their ultimate happiness. This second stage of existence, as the first, was a time of education, of gradually purifying the soul in preparation for the enjoyment of heaven.[45] Chauncy was uncertain, however, as to what specific means of punishment and preparation God would use with recalcitrant sinners in hell. He was convinced only that these additional means would be related to the rational and moral structure of the human creature.[46] Sinners, he wrote, "will be wrought upon, sooner or later, in a moral way, such an one as is adjusted to moral agents, to become righteous persons."[47]

Chauncy anticipated one criticism which any who stood in the Puritan heritage with its emphasis on moral conduct and deep fear of antinomianism would immediately level against his universalism. If all were destined to salvation, did one's behavior in this life really make any difference? The guarantee of ultimate happiness, as Chauncy saw it, did not release humanity from rigorous moral endeavor; belief in universal salvation did not mean sanctioning spiritual license. Punishment even in a finite hell and of limited duration still involved genuine suffering, pain, and torment. But truly moral behavior in this life could either eliminate the necessity of passing through this intermediate stage or minimize the time one would be forced to endure the agony. In his preface to *Salvation for All Men,* he succinctly stated his position:

> And the special advantage of believers above other men is, that they are saved from the wrath to come, saved in the next state, and immediately upon the coming of Christ, are admitted to heavenly happiness. Others must stay for this; being unqualified for such felicity they must wait till they are bro't to a better temper of mind. . . . Believers will be roused to everlasting life at Christ's second coming; that unbelievers will be raised too, but only in order to punish them in hell; and that when their punishments shall have produced a proper effect, they will be recovered to the same happiness with the saints.[48]

In any event, the aim of the benevolent God and the desires of rational humanity were identical and would be fulfilled, for all persons would finally receive eternal happiness in heaven. And when all had attained such happiness, Christ would relinquish his salvific role, and all would enter the eschatological kingdom where God would be "all in all."[49]

When the volume appeared, however, few hurried to praise it. The conservative tone in all the universalist treatises finally made Chauncy's position unacceptable to the Murrayites and others who were in the vanguard of what would become Unitarianism and Universalism in the nineteenth century. The orthodox, of course, smelled heresy and a forsaking of true doctrine. Even Chauncy's allies and friends were reluctant to express their sympathy for his views publicly. When they witnessed the furor that the treatise generated, they knew, perhaps, that the time had not been "seasonable" for its publication.

Chauncy had not intended to undercut the heart of orthodox theology, although that was the effect of his works. As far as he was concerned, he was simply doing for religious doctrine what he had tried to do for religious structures in the Awakening and episcopal controversies and for political order in the Revolutionary era: preserving what he saw as vital to the New England Way by providing a rational and logical defense of present practice and experience. In his own mind he had not destroyed any of the beliefs basic to the New England theology; he had merely restated them in rational form and provided fresh, logical supports "seasonable" to current experience. As Williston Walker commented, one "has the feeling that despite his universalism, Chauncy remained essentially a Calvinist to the end. His doctrine of salvation seems like a revision of the old faith to bring it in harmony with the democratic spirit of the age."[50] Or, as Henry May has argued, Chauncy's presumed radicalism was little more than a moderate Enlightenment rationalism adapted to a Calvinist audience.[51]

Puritans had long spoken of divine sovereignty; Chauncy simply claimed that divine benevolence presented itself as the best manifestation of that sovereignty. Sin still required just punishment, but divine justice and goodness determined that punishment fit both the crime and the criminal by being finite in character. Even predestination was still a useful category to describe God's operation, but divine benevolence meant that all were predestined to salvation. Bringing all creatures to final happiness surely brought more glory to a benevolent and sovereign God than saving some and damning others. Only one orthodox doctrine, that of original sin, was jettisoned, and Chauncy dismissed it not in order to deny the sinfulness of humanity, but to emphasize more strongly the responsibility of individuals for the character and consequences of their conduct. The comments of one reader of "the pudding" would have pleased him. Ebenezer Hazard concluded that the system was "not only rational, but Scriptural . . . and reflects more honour on the divine character than any I have yet met with."[52]

Chauncy himself was not prepared to wage another major battle to defend his stance. He was old and in ill health. His third wife had died in 1783, and while it was rumored two years later that he was courting a forty-year-old widow, he was lonely.[53] His combativeness had diminished with the years. His wishes could no longer determine even the course his flock at First Church would take. Over his objection the congregation decided to part with Puritan tradition and install an organ in their meetinghouse in 1785. That same year, John Clarke, his devoted associate, began to wear a clerical gown in the pulpit despite the good doctor's disapproval.[54] As John Eliot noted, "The Dr. says he will never show any more zeal, or scold, except at vice & immorality."[55] If it had not been "seasonable" to speak of the benevolence of the Deity and of universal salvation, it had become "seasonable" to withdraw from the front lines and allow others to take the lead in shaping and protecting the religious life of New England.

7.

The Seasonable Puritan

When his universalist bombshell struck New England, Charles Chauncy was approaching his eightieth year. So long as he was physically able, he maintained a keen interest in developments both religious and secular, but in his declining years he was forced to curtail his active participation in many affairs. One political dispute did claim some of his attention, however. In 1780 while Massachusetts was in the process of formulating its first state constitution, Chauncy endorsed its most controversial provision, the third article of the Bill of Rights which authorized the use of public tax monies to subsidize salaries of teachers of religion and morals. Attacks on Article III were numerous, ranging from claims that the provision would legally establish the dominant Congregationalism to fears that it would impede the free exercise of religious liberty in matters of personal belief and practice. Chauncy himself was criticized in the public press for his position, especially by Baptist spokesman Isaac Backus, but remained firm in his support.[1]

As was so often the case, Chauncy's motivation was essentially conservative, stemming from a desire to protect the status which religion had long enjoyed in the former Bay Colony. To provide formal means to secure ministers' salaries would ensure the health of organized religion. Of course Chauncy must have realized that the Congregationalism which he served would reap the greatest benefits from enactment of the proposal, but Congregationalism, however fragmented it may have become, was that form of Christianity which had nurtured Massachusetts religious life for nearly two centuries and stood as a symbol of religious truth for generations of New Englanders.

Chauncy also maintained his longstanding concern for educational activities in his last years. His name appeared as a subscriber to one of the first maps of the New England region published after independence, and the year before his death he pledged four guineas to Yale College, now headed by his friend Ezra Stiles, for the purchase of new equipment.[2] In 1785 when the now distinguished American Academy of Arts and Sciences was organized, the venerable senior pastor of Old Brick became a charter member.[3] It had been a long road from the days as a young scholar at Harvard to recognition as one of the leading intellectuals of the new nation. "He was eminent for his talents, learning, and love of liberty, civil and religious," went the description of Chauncy when his portrait was hung in the Massachusetts Historical Society gallery.[4] He would have been pleased to know he was regarded as learned.

By 1786, though, age had begun to take its toll, and Chauncy's health began to falter. He died February 10, 1787. At the memorial service for Chauncy, John Clarke singled out personal piety and diligent study as the two primary characteristics of the deceased preacher's life style.[5] Both required a strong sense of discipline and the will to order one's life carefully. Perhaps it was this firm appreciation of the old Puritan emphasis on self-discipline that earned Chauncy the respect of his peers. The disciplined regimen of even his personal habits was well known among his colleagues. In one early biographical sketch, the author recounted: "At twelve o'clock he [Chauncy] took one pinch of snuff, and only one in twenty-four hours. At one o'clock, he dined on one dish of plain wholesome food, and after dinner, took one glass of wine, and one pipe of tobacco, and only one in twenty-four hours."[6]

It was not enough to order just one's religious habits; every dimension of life needed to be brought under control. Chauncy's sense of discipline extended into the realm of family relationships. For example, "when grandchildren visited his study, he would teach them self-discipline by scattering raisins on the floor and making them wait an improving length of time before giving the signal to scramble."[7] The old man may have been regarded by some as a renegade for his modifications of Puritan theology, but he never abandoned the Puritan belief that discipline would strengthen both soul and body.

That discipline, though, bred a strong sense of self-assurance, particularly when Chauncy played the role of combatant in controversy. Ebenezer Parkman, who watched Chauncy's dander rise during the Awakening era, occasionally was made "uncomfortable by his Coarseness and unhandsome Conduct" in attacking New Light opponents.[8] Eleazar Wheelock, who felt Chauncy's ire when each sought to gain advantage for the educational institution he represented, noted the "sarcastical and savage" manner in which Chauncy dealt with those who disagreed with him.[9] But Chauncy may have recognized that his own commitment to what he regarded as right and his extreme self-confidence from time to time led to overstatement and excess of expression. As Loyalist Peter Oliver described him:

> Dr. *Chauncy* . . . was a man of Sense, but of exorbitant Passions; he would utter Things in Conversation that bordered too near upon Blasphemy, & when such wild Expressions were noticed to him, by observing that his Sermons were free from such Extravagances, he would reply, that "in making his Sermons he always kept a Blotter by him." He was of a very resentfull, unforgiving Temper; & when he was in the Excess of his Passion, a Bystander would naturally judge that he had been educated in the Purlieus of *Bedlam;* but he was open in all his Actions.[10]

Chauncy's discipline, while he was confident it would lead to eternal bliss, was harnessed towards one goal on this earth: the protection and strengthening of the New England Way. Chauncy always sought to preserve traditional structures, whether in religion or politics. Of course, such an endeavor is a classic human response to perceived threats to established institutions and ways of doing things. In the Awakening, Chauncy defended the structure of the standing order and the use of the "means of grace" in striving for salvation in response to what he saw as the potential destructiveness of itineracy and stress on an immediate and assured experience of conversion in the evangelical approach. When Chauncy attacked the plan to establish an Anglican episcopate in the colonies, he was again reacting to a presumed threat, the potential challenge an episcopal structure might hurl at the presbyterian/congregational patterns operative in New England and the possible demolition of the Puritan hegemony in New England religious life which an established Church of England might have the power to effect.

At the time of the independence movement, Chauncy became an enthusiastic supporter of the American cause because he became convinced that changes in British policy signalled the end of that liberty which the colonists thought they once possessed. And in his universalist writings, the aging pastor again attempted to preserve the theological categories and constructs he believed central to Protestant belief from presumed disintegration at the hands of both evangelicals and unscriptural rationalists.

But Chauncy's conservative efforts did not mean he was inextricably bound to the past or even to the status quo. As strongly as he was committed to preserving institutions and structures hallowed by time, he was devoted to modifying the supports which undergirded them in order to make them fit for service in a changing time. The universalist treatises are perhaps the most obvious case in point, for while Chauncy did make some rather striking alterations in the way the doctrine of election and the matter of sin were to be explained, he nevertheless generally continued to use traditional theological categories and to base his work, as Puritans had always done, on a reasoned explication of Scripture. But securing his form of belief from erosion required modifications in the usual interpretation of several doctrines.

In both the universalist writings and the numerous anti-Awakening works, Chauncy had spoken of the experience of conversion so central to Puritan religious style, but offered an understanding of Christian nurture and growth in grace through sustained religious practice which broadened the idea of precisely what constituted conversion. Yet many no longer underwent a discrete experience of conversion, and Chauncy's reasoned reworking of the way conversion occurred presented a form of support to those who saw their own spiritual lives as a process of gradual development in holiness. Even in the political arena, Chauncy was willing to alter tactics when old forms appeared unlikely to preserve the structures he thought worthy of continued life. His shift from calling for loyalty to the crown, use of petition, and practice of nonviolent protest to endorsing active rebellion and military resistance was not a change of fundamental principles, but one necessary to render those embryonic American symbols of liberty safe from destruction by an increasingly corrupt Parliament. Whenever Chauncy proposed modifications in traditional belief or shifted modes of tactical behavior, he was guided by a desire to buttress what he saw as right and proper in a way "seasonable" to time and circumstance without shattering the foundations of the established order.

In his own lifetime, Chauncy found Jonathan Edwards his most formidable opponent. Edwards in life confronted Chauncy in his first major controversy over the merits of the Awakening. Edwards in death, through his writings, provided Chauncy with material to combat and counter in his last major work, the *Five Dissertations on the Scripture Account of the Fall.* Edwards clearly had the keener, more original mind and in the

Awakening era received more public sympathy than Chauncy. But the defender of the revivals and what he believed to be orthodox Calvinism suffered serious setbacks in his efforts to make the evangelical spirit normative for eighteenth century American Puritan expression. He was dismissed from his pulpit in Northampton, relegated to a wilderness outpost as missionary to the Indians, and died an early death in a smallpox epidemic when, as president of Princeton, he had finally been restored to a position in which he could exert considerable influence on the contemporary religious scene. Edwards's stature today results largely from the recovery of appreciation for his brilliance among students of colonial thought. But he also acquired a large number of disciples, pastors and teachers who shared his religious commitment and zeal but not his depth and who wound up transforming his creativity into scholastic rigidity.

Chauncy has attracted few contemporary admirers; even less in his own day did he attract a devoted band of followers eager to propagate his viewpoint, though he did not lack comrades or ideological compatriots. Yet Chauncy's contributions to American religious life stand as significant as those of Edwards. His challenge to evangelicalism enabled a more rationalistic form of religious belief and practice to enter the mainstream of American religion. His efforts to combine fresh examination of doctrinal supports with orthodox affirmation not only aided the birth of Unitarianism, but helped determine the continuing theological task. His adamant opposition to presumed threats to religious liberty, if an Anglican bishopric were established in America, and to political liberty, if shifts in British colonial policy carried the day, partially shaped the understanding of liberty which his fellow citizens sought to institutionalize in the new United States.

If history has not yet accorded him the status he deserves as defender and advocate, the failure perhaps stems from the fact that both his words and his works issued as specific responses to particular crises and controversies which marked eighteenth century American life. In retrospect, they may seem so bound to those crises and controversies that it is easy to overlook their larger significance. Chauncy himself might have understood, for he knew that he always acted in ways he believed "seasonable" to the times. What became "seasonable" to other times differed from what was "seasonable" to his own time. But for eighteenth century America, Charles Chauncy remains the "seasonable" Puritan.

Notes

PREFACE

1. Douglass Adair and John A. Schutz, eds., *Peter Oliver's Origin and Progress of the American Revolution: A Tory View* (San Marino, Calif.: Huntington Library, 1963), p. 44n.

2. Ibid., p. 92.

CHAPTER 1

1. Charles Chauncy, "Life of the Rev. President (Charles) Chauncy, Written at the Request of Dr. Stiles, May 23, 1768," 1 *Collections* Massachusetts Historical Society, 10 (Boston: Munroe, Francis and Parker, 1809), pp. 171–80.

2. See his *God's Mercy, Shewed to His People in Giving Them a Faithful Ministry and Schools of Learning . . .* (Cambridge: Samuel Green, 1655).

3. All dates are New Style.

4. Chauncy had been outraged at finding his great-grandfather's papers destroyed when writing the biographical sketch for Stiles and determined to destroy his own papers, creating for later historians the same problem he encountered. See his "Life of the Rev. President (Charles) Chauncy," p. 179.

5. College Papers, Harvard University Archives, 1, p. 66, item 142.

6. Clifford K. Shipton, *Sibley's Harvard Graduates,* 6 (Boston: For the Massachusetts Historical Society, 1942), pp. 439–67, includes a capsule of Chauncy's college days.

7. William Tudor, *The Life of James Otis of Massachusetts* (Boston: Wells and Lilly, 1823), p. 149.

8. Shipton, p. 444.

9. Conrad Wright, *The Beginnings of Unitarianism in America* (Boston: Beacon Press, 1955), p. 37.

10. Shipton, p. 440.

11. Larzer Ziff, *Puritanism in America* (New York: Viking Press, 1973), pp. 197–202. It was not unknown for clergy to refuse to participate in or attend the ordination of one with whom they disagreed. For example, many were so wary of the opinions of Jonathan Mayhew, Chauncy's close friend, that the West Church wisely chose not to invite most of the Boston clergy to his ordination and spared their new pastor embarrassment if they declined to attend.

12. *Records of the First Church in Boston, Publications* Colonial Society of Massachusetts, 39 (Boston: Colonial Society of Massachusetts, 1961), p. 152.

13. This sketch follows Carl Bridenbaugh, *Cities in the Wilderness: Urban Life in America, 1625–1742* (New York: Capricorn Books, 1964; first pub., 1938), part 3.

14. *Records of the First Church in Boston,* pp. 159, 161–62, 172–73, 213–14.

15. The classic study is Edmund S. Morgan, *The Puritan Family,* rev. ed. (New York: Harper and Row, 1966), but also see John Demos, *A Little Commonwealth: Family Life in Plymouth Colony* (London and New York: Oxford University Press, 1970).

16. May 13, 1737, entry in the "Diary of the Rev. Thomas Prince," *Publications* Colonial Society of Massachusetts, 19 (Boston: Colonial Society of Massachusetts, 1918), p. 345.

17. *Records of the First Church in Boston,* pp. 154–55.

18. Boston Registry Department, *Records Relating to the Early History of Boston,* 24: *A Report of the Record Commissioners of the City of Boston: Boston Births from 1700 to 1800* (Boston: Rockwell and Churchill, 1894), pp. 191, 201, 211.

19. Barney L. Jones, "Charles Chauncy and the Great Awakening in New England" (unpublished Ph.D. dissertation, Duke University, 1958), p. 29.

20. Robert F. Seybolt, "The Ministers at the Town Meeting in Colonial Boston," *Publications* Colonial Society of Massachusetts, 32 (Boston: Colonial Society of Massachusetts, 1937), p. 301.

21. Boston Registry Department, *Records Relating to the Early History of Boston,* 15: *A Report of the Record Commissioners of the City of Boston, Containing the Records of Boston Selectmen, 1736 to 1742* (Boston: Rockwell and Churchill, 1886), p. 4.

22. See "Diary of the Rev. Samuel Checkley, 1735," *Publications* Colonial Society of Massachusetts, 12 (Boston: Colonial Society of Massachusetts, 1911), pp. 297–300, 303, 306; "Diary of Rev. Samuel Cooper, of Boston," *New England Historical and Genealogical Register,* 41 (1887): 389; "Diary of Samuel Cooper, 1775–1776," ed. Frederick Tuckerman, *American Historical Review,* 6 (1901): 340–41; "Diary of the Rev. Thomas Prince," pp. 337, 348, 359, 361; *Letters and Diary of John Rowe, Boston Merchant, 1759–1762, 1764–1779,* ed. Anne Rowe Cunningham (Boston: W.B. Clarke, 1903), pp. 83, 92, 103, 130, 306; and "Diary of Samuel Sewall," 5 *Collections* Massachusetts Historical Society, 7 (Boston: For the Massachusetts Historical Society, 1882), pp. 345, 356.

23. May 27, 1731 Subscription for Support of Josiah Cotton (Harvard College 1722) in Ministry at Providence, Rhode Island, Colman Papers, Massachusetts Historical Society; Clifford K. Shipton, *Sibley's Harvard Graduates,* 7 (Boston: For the Massachusetts Historical Society, 1945), pp. 50–56.

24. See *The Case and Complaint of Mr. Samuel Osborn* (Boston: W. McAlpine, 1743).

25. See Shipton, 6: 304–8.

26. Charles Chauncy, "A Sketch of Eminent Men in New-England," 1 *Collections* Massachusetts Historical Society, 10 (Boston: Munroe, Francis and Parker, 1809), p. 162.

27. November 8, 1734 letter from Timothy Cutler to Zachary Gray, Emmet Collection, New York Public Library.

28. *The Character and Overthrow of Laish Considered and Applied* (Boston: S. Kneeland and T. Green, 1734).

29. *Man's Life Considered under the Similitude of Vapour, That Appeareth for a Little Time, and Then Vanisheth Away* (Boston: B. Green, 1731), and *Early Piety Recommended and Exemplified* (Boston: S. Kneeland and T. Green, 1732).

30. *Nathanael's Character Display'd* (Boston: n.p., 1733).

31. *Prayer for Help a Seasonable Duty Upon the Ceasing of Godly and Faithful Men* (Boston: T. Fleet, 1737).

32. *New England Weekly Journal,* January 23, 1739.

33. *Records of the First Church in Boston,* pp. 184–85. The funds came from Mrs. Chauncy's estate, and the church agreed to allow the Chauncys to live in the parsonage for at least five years after Mrs. Chauncy completed the remodelling.

CHAPTER 2

1. *The Great Awakening in New England* (New York: Harper and Row, 1957), pp. 2–3. Also see William G. McLoughlin, *New England Dissent, 1630–1833: The Baptists and the Separation of Church and State,* 2 vols. (Cambridge: Harvard University Press, 1971), vol. 1, p. 332.

2. Charles H. Lippy, "Seasonable Revolutionary: Charles Chauncy and the Ideology of Liberty" (unpublished Ph.D. dissertation, Princeton University, 1972), pp. 110–36.

3. See *An Account of the Rise, Progress and Consequences of the Land Bank; and the Silver Schemes in the Province of the Massachusetts-Bay* (Boston: n.p., 1744); and George Athan Billias, *The Massachusetts Land Bankers of 1740,* University of Maine Studies, 2nd ser., no. 74 (Orono: University of Maine Press, 1959), an important corrective to John C. Miller, "Religion, Finance, and Democracy in Massachusetts," *New England Quarterly,* 6 (1933): 29–58.

4. See, for example, Perry Miller, "Jonathan Edwards and the Great Awakening," in his *Errand Into the Wilderness* (Cambridge: Harvard University Press, 1956), pp. 153–66; and Alan Heimert, *Religion and the American Mind: From the Great Awakening to the Revolution* (Cambridge: Harvard University Press, 1966).

5. See Richard F. Bushman, *From Puritan to Yankee: Character and the Social Order in Connecticut, 1690–1765* (Cambridge: Harvard University Press, 1967), pp. 187–95; McLoughlin, pp. 329–39; and H. Richard Niebuhr, *The Kingdom of God in America* (New York: Harper and Bros., 1937), pp. 135–50.

6. Bushman, passim; McLoughlin, p. 333n.

7. *Boston Weekly News-Letter,* September 25, 1740.

8. The standard study, Gaustad's *The Great Awakening in New England,* pp. 80–101, contains a detailed analysis of the Edwards-Chauncy disputes. Also see Charles H. Lippy, "The Great Awakening: An Opponent's Perspective," *Ohio Journal of Religious Studies,* 2:1 (1974): 44–52.

9. See, respectively, Heimert, passim; Conrad Wright, *The Begin-*

nings of Unitarianism in America (Boston: Beacon Press, 1955); and G. Adolf Koch, *Republican Religion: The American Revolution and the Cult of Reason* (New York: Henry Holt and Co., 1933), pp. 191–95.

10. Perry Miller, *Jonathan Edwards* (New York: W. Sloane Associates, 1949), p. 167. On Edwards's understanding of the sensible, see Roland A. Delattre, *Beauty and Sensibility in the Thought of Jonathan Edwards* (New Haven: Yale University Press, 1968).

11. Jonathan Edwards, *A Treatise Concerning Religious Affections,* ed. John E. Smith, *The Works of Jonathan Edwards,* 2 (New Haven: Yale University Press, 1959), p. 96; Arthur C. McGiffert, Jr., *Jonathan Edwards* (New York: Harper and Bros., 1932), p. 74.

12. See Jonathan Edwards, *Treatise on Grace & Other Posthumous Writings,* ed. Paul Helm (Cambridge and London: James Clarke and Co., Ltd., 1971), pp. 54–56, and his *Religious Affections,* p. 96.

13. April 2, 1770 letter from Charles Chauncy to Ezra Stiles, Stiles Papers, Yale University.

14. Chauncy's belief in the gracious work of God as a continuing process later took him far astray from the mainstream of covenant theology, although he never abandoned belief in the efficacy and adequacy of the practical structures rooted in that theology. See chapter 6 above.

15. *Enthusiasm Described and Caution'd Against* (Boston: J. Draper for S. Eliot and J. Blanchard, 1742), p. 5.

16. *Seasonable Thoughts on the State of Religion in New-England, a Treatise in Five Parts* (Boston: Rogers and Fowle for S. Eliot, 1743), pp. 97–99.

17. Ironically, it was Solomon Stoddard, Edwards's grandfather, who had first encouraged the view that the Lord's Supper was a general "means of grace" rather than a sacrament reserved for full church members.

18. *The Only Compulsion Proper to Be Made Use of in the Affairs of Conscience and Religion* (Boston: J. Draper for J. Edwards, 1739), p. 15. Chauncy articulated the same position nearly forty years later in his one major work on the sacraments, *"Breaking of Bread," in Remembrance of the Dying Love of Christ, a Gospel Institution* (Boston: Printed for Thomas Leverett, 1777).

19. *The New Creature Describ'd and Consider'd as the Sure Characteristick of a Man's Being in Christ* (Boston: G. Rogers for J. Edwards and S. Eliot, 1741), pp. 23–25.

20. *The Gifts of the Spirit to Ministers Consider'd in Their Diversity* (Boston: Rogers and Fowle, 1742), pp. 14–15.

21. Ibid., p. 6.

22. Ibid., p. 8.

23. *New Creature,* pp. 21–33.

24. *The Out-Pouring of the Holy Ghost* (Boston: T. Fleet for D. Henchman and S. Eliot, 1742), pp. 33–46.

25. *Seasonable Thoughts,* pp. 274–81.

26. "Extracts from the Private Journal of the Rev. Mr. Ebenezer Parkman of Westborough, Massachusetts," in Joseph Tracy, *The Great Awakening* (Boston: Tappan and Dennet, 1842), p. 208.

27. Ibid., p. 361.

28. Itinerant Gilbert Tennant's well-known sermon, *The Danger of an Unconverted Ministry, Considered in a Sermon on Mark VI, 34* (Philadelphia: Benjamin Franklin, 1740), had earlier presented the same challenge to the settled clergy.

29. Tracy, p. 209.

30. Ibid.

31. *Enthusiasm Describ'd,* pp. iii–iv. Chauncy's dislike for such "unseasonable" criticism and its implicit challenge to the position of esteem to which the Massachusetts clergy had long been accustomed may have prompted the publication of his Thursday lecture, *An Unbridled Tongue A Sure Evidence, that Our Religion is Hypocritical and Vain* (Boston: Rogers and Fowle, 1741), in which he blasted those who spoke falsehoods in the interest of religion. The same day Chauncy delivered *An Unbridled Tongue,* Jonathan Edwards preached his revival apology, *The Distinguishing Marks of a Work of the Spirit of God,* at Yale.

32. *A Letter from A Gentleman in Boston to Mr. George Wishart, One of the Ministers of Edinburgh, Concerning the State of Religion in New-England* (Edinburgh: n.p., 1742), esp. pp. 8–9, 13–14, 21–23.

33. *Enthusiasm Describ'd,* pp. iii–iv.

34. Ibid., p. 12.

35. For example, see the September 14, 1743 letter from Isaac Watts to Benjamin Colman, "Letters of Dr. Watts," 2 *Proceedings,* Massachusetts Historical Society, 9 (Boston: For the Society, 1895), p. 400.

36. *Seasonable Thoughts,* pp. 55–57.

37. Ibid., 101ff.

38. Edward M. Griffin, "A Biography of Charles Chauncy (1705–1787)" (unpublished Ph.D. dissertation, Stanford University, 1966), pp. 87–90. Also see Barney L. Jones, "Charles Chauncy and the Great Awakening in New England" (unpublished Ph.D. dissertation, Duke University, 1958), pp. 51–52.

39. Tracy, pp. 287–302. Also see Ebenezer Parkman, *Journal of Ebenezer Parkman* (Westborough, Mass.: n.p., 1906), p. 72.

40. James Davenport, *The Reverend Mr. James Davenport's Confession & Retractions* (Boston: S. Kneeland and T. Green, 1744), pp. 3–8. The forces leading to congregational schisms were, of course, more complex, although attitudes towards the Awakening were an important ingredient. For a careful study, see C. C. Goen, *Revivalism and Separatism in New England, 1740–1800: Strict Congregationalists and Separate Baptists in the Great Awakening* (New Haven: Yale University Press, 1962).

41. Quoted in William H. Sumner, *History of East Boston* (Boston: J. E. Tilton & Co., 1858), p. 266.

42. See George Whitefield, *A Letter to the Reverend Mr. Chauncy, on Account of Some Passages Relating to the Revd. Mr. Whitefield, in His Book Intitled* [sic] *Seasonable Thoughts . . .* (Boston: S. Kneeland and T. Green, 1745). Chauncy replied with *A Letter to the Reverend Mr. George Whitefield, Vindicating Certain Pasages He Has Excepted against, in a Late Book Entitled Seasonable Thoughts . . .* (Boston: Rogers and Fowle for S. Eliot, 1745). There is no extant copy of Chauncy's earlier diatribe against Whitefield, *A Letter to The Reverend Mr. George Whitefield, Publickly Calling upon Him to Vindicate His Conduct, or Confess His Faults* (Boston: T. Fleet, 1743).

43. "Correspondence between Rev. Thomas Prince and Rev. Charles Chauncy," 4 *Collections* Massachusetts Historical Society, 4 (Boston: For the Society, 1854), p. 239.

44. *Ministers Exhorted and Encouraged to Take Heed to Themselves, and to Their Doctrine* (Boston: Rogers and Fowle for S. Eliot, 1744), esp. pp. 7–15, 19–21, 30.

45. *Ministers Cautioned against the Occasions of Contempt* (Boston: Rogers and Fowle for S. Eliot, 1744).

46. *Main Currents in American Thought,* 3 vols. (New York: Harcourt, Brace, and Co., 1927–30), vol. 1, pp. 148–62.

47. The themes are developed in Miller's *Jonathan Edwards* and his "Jonathan Edwards and the Great Awakening."

48. *Religion and the American Mind,* esp. pp. 2–20. Heimert did note the social conservatism of those who opposed the Awakening.

49. Robert F. Seybolt, "The Ministers at the Town Meeting in Colonial Boston," *Publications* Colonial Society of Massachusetts, 32 (Boston: Colonial Society of Massachusetts, 1937), p. 301; Boston Registry Department, *Records Relating to the Early History of Boston,* 17: *A Report of the Record Commissioners of the City of Boston, Containing the Selectmen's Minutes from 1742–3 to 1753* (Boston: Rockwell and Churchill, 1887), p. 71.

CHAPTER 3

1. Faculty Records, Harvard University Archives, 1, p. 251.

2. The standard biographies of Mayhew are Charles W. Akers, *Called unto Liberty: A Life of Jonathan Mayhew, 1720–1766* (Cambridge: Harvard University Press, 1964), and Alden Bradford, *Memoir of the Life and Writings of Rev. Jonathan Mayhew, D.D., Pastor of the West Church and Society in Boston, From June, 1747, to July, 1766* (Boston: C.C. Little & Co., 1838).

3. Jonathan Mayhew, *Seven Sermons* (Boston: Rogers and Fowle, 1749), esp. pp. 42–58. Also see McMurry S. Richey, "Jonathan Mayhew: American Christian Rationalist," in *A Miscellany of American Christianity,* ed. Stuart C. Henry (Durham: Duke University Press, 1963), pp. 310–15.

4. Mayhew, *Seven Sermons,* pp. 70–73.

5. Jonathan Mayhew, *Two Discourses Delivered November 23d. 1758* (Boston: Edes and Gill, 1758), p. 10.

6. *A Sermon Preach'd in the Audience of His Excellency William Shirley, Esq. . . .* (Boston: Samuel Kneeland, 1754), p. 28.

7. Jonathan Mayhew, "A Discourse Concerning Unlimited Submission and Non-Resistance to the Higher Powers," *Pamphlets of the American Revolution, 1750–76,* 1, ed. Bernard Bailyn (Cambridge: Belknap Press of Harvard University, 1965), p. 232.

8. [Charles Lee], "Strictures on a Pamphlet, Entitled, a 'Friendly Address to All Reasonable Americans on the Subject of Our Political Confusions' " (1774), *Collections* New York Historical Society, 4 (New York: Printed for the Society, 1872), p. 153, claimed that 99 percent of Americans thought Charles I had been a tyrant.

9. Conrad Wright, *The Beginnings of Unitarianism in America* (Boston: Beacon Press, 1955), p. 67.

10. *The Counsel of Two Confederate Kings to Set the Son of Tabeal on the Throne, Represented as Evil, in It's Natural Tendency and Moral Aspect* (Boston: D. Gookin, 1746), pp. 32ff.

11. Ibid., pp. 41–42.

12. *"Marvellous Things Done by the Right Hand and Holy Arm of God in Getting Him the Victory"* (Boston: T. Fleet, 1745).

13. See the June 14, 1745; August 4, 1745; October 29, 1745; January 14, 1746; and February 14, 1746 letters from Chauncy to Pepperrell in *The Pepperrell Papers, 6 Collections* Massachusetts Historical Society, 10 (Boston: For the Society, 1899).

14. *Civil Magistrates Must Be Just, Ruling in the Fear of God* (Boston: Printed by Order of the Honourable House of Representatives, 1747), pp. 38–41. At this time, there was apparently some difficulty in securing adequate voluntary contributions for the First Church clergy, for Chauncy and Foxcroft had to ask their congregation to "pitch upon some method" to raise money to pay them. See Hamilton A. Hill, *History of Old South Church (Third Church) Boston, 1669–1884,* 2 vols. (Boston and New York: Houghton, Mifflin, 1890), vol. 1, pp. 580–81.

15. Quoted in "Address in Opposition to Issuing More Paper Money," *Letter-Book of Samuel Sewall, 6 Collections* Massachusetts Historical Society, 2 (Boston: For the Society, 1888), p. 237n.

16. *Civil Magistrates,* p. 17.

17. Ibid., pp. 32–37.

18. Ibid., p. 54. Martha L. Counts, "The Political Views of the Eighteenth Century New England Clergy as Expressed in Their Election Sermons" (unpublished Ph.D. dissertation, Columbia University, 1956), pp. 85–86, called Chauncy's outline on protection of rights as the duty of the ruler the most comprehensive statement on the subject in any eighteenth century Massachusetts election discourse.

19. February 14, 1746 letter from Chauncy to William Pepperrell, *Pepperrell Papers,* pp. 446–47.

20. Clifford K. Shipton, *Sibley's Harvard Graduates,* 8 (Boston: For the Massachusetts Historical Society, 1951), p. 63, based on the May 4, 1731, entry in the Ebenezer Bridge Diary, Harvard College Library; Barney L. Jones, "Charles Chauncy and the Great Awakening in New England" (unpublished Ph.D. dissertation, Duke University, 1958), p. 90.

21. The ambivalence in early Puritan attitudes is admirably appraised in Francis Jennings, *The Invasion of America: Indians, Colonialism, and the Cant of Conquest* (Chapel Hill: University of North Carolina Press for the Institute of Early American History and Culture, 1975).

22. Gideon Hawley, "A Letter from Rev. Gideon Hawley of Marshpec Containing a Narrative of His Journey to Onohoghwage in July, 1753," *Ecclesiastical Records, State of New York,* ed. E.T. Corwin, 5 (Albany: J.B. Lyon, 1901), pp. 399–405.

23. *The Idle-Poor Secluded from the Bread of Charity by the Christian Law* (Boston: Thomas Fleet, 1752).

24. Alan Heimert, *Religion and the American Mind: From the Great Awakening to the Revolution* (Cambridge: Harvard University Press, 1966), p. 248.

25. *Idle-Poor,* pp. 8–12.

26. Ibid., p. 13.

27. *Christian Love, as Exemplified by the First Christian Church in Their Having All Things in Common, Placed in Its True and Just Point of Light* (Boston: Thomas Leverett, 1773), esp. p. 19.

28. Boston Registry Department, *Records Relating to the Early History of Boston,* 19: *A Report of the Record Commissioners of the City of Boston, Containing the Selectmen's Minutes from 1754 through 1763* (Boston: Rockwell and Churchill, 1887), pp. 9–10; Robert F. Seybolt, *The Public Schools of Colonial Boston, 1635–1775* (Cambridge: Harvard University Press, 1935), p. 91; Robert F. Seybolt, "The Ministers at the Town Meeting in Colonial Boston," *Publications* Colonial Society of Massachusetts, 32 (Boston: Colonial Society of Massachusetts, 1937), p. 301.

29. Boston: Thomas Fleet, 1754.

30. Clifford K. Shipton, *Sibley's Harvard Graduates,* 6 (Boston: For the Massachusetts Historical Society, 1942), p. 450.

31. *Earthquakes a Token of the Righteous Anger of God* (Boston: Edes and Gill, 1755).

32. *A Letter to a Friend, Giving a Concise, but Just Account, According to the Advice Hitherto Received, of the Ohio-Defeat* (Boston: Edes and Gill, 1755).

33. Richard Slotkin, *Regeneration Through Violence: The Mythology of the American Frontier, 1600–1860* (Middletown, Conn.: Wesleyan University Press, 1973), pp. 228–29.

34. *A Second Letter to a Friend; Giving a More Particular Narrative of the Defeat of the French Army at Lake-George, by the New-England Troops, than Has Yet Been Published* (Boston: Edes and Gill, 1755).

35. *The Earth Delivered from the Curse to Which It Is, at Present, Subjected* (Boston: Edes and Gill, 1756).

36. John Taylor, *The Scripture Doctrine of Original Sin, Proposed to a Free and Candid Examination* (London: Printed for the Author by J. Wilson, 1740).

37. William Chauncey Fowler, "President Charles Chauncey and His Ancestors and Descendants," *New England Historical and Genealogical Register,* 10 (1856): 335.

38. Samuel Webster, *A Winter Evening's Conversation upon the Doctrine of Original Sin* (New Haven: Reprinted by James Parker, 1757).

39. The best edition of Edwards's treatise is *Original Sin,* ed. Clyde A. Holbrook, *The Works of Jonathan Edwards,* 3 (New Haven: Yale University Press, 1970).

40. Peter Clark, *The Scripture-Doctrine of Original Sin Stated and Defended. A Summer Morning's Conversation between a Minister and a Neighbor* (Boston: S. Kneeland, 1758).

41. *The Opinion of One That Has Perused the Summer Morning's Conversation, Concerning Original Sin, Wrote by the Rev. Mr. Peter Clark* (Boston: Green & Russell, 1758), p. 16.

42. Ibid., pp. 26–27.

43. *Earth Delivered,* pp. 18–22.

44. *Records of the First Church in Boston, Publications* Colonial Society of Massachusetts, 39 (Boston: Colonial Society of Massachusetts, 1961), p. 218.

45. Ms. Diary of Andrew Eliot, Massachusetts Historical Society.

46. Clifford K. Shipton, *Sibley's Harvard Graduates,* 7 (Boston: For the Massachusetts Historical Society, 1945), p. 787; December 3, 1761 and December 21, 1761 letters from Charles Chauncy to Ezra Stiles, Stiles Papers, Yale University.

47. Rufus P. Stebbins, *A Centennial Discourse Delivered to the First Congregational Church and Society in Leominster, September 24, 1843* (Boston: C.C. Little and J. Brown, 1843); Shipton, 6, pp. 190–96.

48. June 15, 1761, July 21, 1761, and August 8, 1761, letters from Chauncy to Ezra Stiles, Stiles Papers.

49. E.H. Gillett, "President Wheelock and Dr. Chauncy," *American Presbyterian Review,* 3rd ser., 11 (1871): 463–75.

50. William C. Lane, "New Hampshire's Part in Restoring the Library and Apparatus of Harvard College after the Fire of 1764," *Publications* Colonial Society of Massachusetts, 25 (Boston: Colonial Society of Massachusetts, 1924), pp. 24–33.

51. See the June 28, 1761, letter from Chauncy to Shute Shrimpton Yeamans, Washburn Papers, Massachusetts Historical Society; Ulrich B. Phillips, "An Antigua Plantation," *North Carolina Historical Review,* 3 (1926): 439–45; the April 21, 1785 report of a committee to arbitrate Charles Chauncy's claim to one-third interest in the Antigua sugar plantation held by his late wife, and accounts dated April 30, 1783, December 31, 1783, and July 4, 1785, of Chauncy with Messers. Rob., Rob., & Ebenz. Maitland, Greenough Papers, Massachusetts Historical Society.

CHAPTER 4

1. Edmund S. and Helen M. Morgan, *The Stamp Act Crisis: Prologue to Revolution* (Chapel Hill: University of North Carolina Press for the Institute of Early American History and Culture, 1953), p. 275, and Edmund S. Morgan, "Colonial Ideas of Parliamentary Power, 1764–1766," *The Reinterpretation of the American Revolution,* ed. Jack P. Greene (New York: Harper and Row, 1968), pp. 151–81, deny that any Americans made this distinction. My reading of the materials, however, suggests otherwise. To be sure, not all colonial writers set up the problem in this fashion, but some did. See, for example, Jared Ingersoll, *Mr. Ingersoll's Letters Relating to the Stamp-Act* (New Haven: Samuel Green, 1766), pp. 11–16. One widely read pamphleteer who did deny the distinction was John Dickinson. See *John Dickinson's Farmer's Letters* (Philadelphia: n.p., 1801), pp. 19–20.

2. *Farmer's Letters,* pp. 22–26.

3. Samuel Adams ("Candidus"), *Boston Gazette,* October 20, 1772.

4. *Farmer's Letters,* p. 13.

5. Daniel Dulaney, "Considerations on the Propriety of Imposing Taxes in the British Colonies, for the Purpose of Raising a Revenue" (1765), *Pamphlets of the American Revolution, 1750–76,* 1, ed. Bernard Bailyn (Cambridge: Belknap Press of Harvard University, 1965), 632.

6. "A Vindication of the British Colonies against the Aspersions of the Halifax Gentleman, in His Letters to a Rhode-Island Friend"

(1765), *Pamphlets of the American Revolution,* 1, pp. 564, 576–77.

7. *Letters to the Ministry from Governor Bernard, General Gage, and Commodore Hood* (Salem: Samuel Hall, 1769), p. 58.

8. "Considerations on the Propriety of Imposing Taxes," p. 632.

9. Jonathan Mayhew, *The Snare Broken* (Boston: Edes and Gill, 1766).

10. *A Thanksgiving Sermon Preach'd at Pepperrell, July 24th, 1766* (Boston: Edes and Gill, 1766).

11. *A Discourse on "the Good News from a Far Country"* (Boston: Kneeland and Adams, 1766), pp. 7–8.

12. Ibid., pp. 9–13.

13. Ibid., p. 14.

14. Ibid., p. 24.

15. "Letters from Andrew Eliot to Thomas Hollis," 4 *Collections* Massachusetts Historical Society, 4 (Boston: For the Society, 1858), pp. 404, 420–21.

16. Alan Heimert, *Religion and the American Mind: From the Great Awakening to the Revolution* (Cambridge: Harvard University Press, 1966), pp. 144–45.

17. The standard treatments of the Episcopal Controversy are Carl Bridenbaugh, *Mitre and Sceptre: Transatlantic Faiths, Ideas, Personalities, and Politics, 1689–1775* (New York: Oxford University Press, 1962), and Arthur L. Cross, *The Anglican Episcopate and the American Colonies* (New York and London: Longmans, Green, 1902).

18. *Magnalia Christi Americana,* 2 vols. (Hartford: Silas Andrus, 1820), vol. 2, p. 219.

19. Some consideration was given to the establishment of an American episcopate during the reign of Queen Anne, but her Hanoverian successors were not of the high church persuasion which was most interested in extending episcopacy to the colonies and therefore tended to ignore the religious situation of American Anglicanism.

20. See Winthrop S. Hudson, *Religion in America* (New York: Charles Scribner's Sons, 1965), pp. 87–92; Frederick V. Mills, "Anglican Expansion in Colonial America, 1761–1776," *Historical Magazine of the Protestant Episcopal Church,* 39 (1970): 315–24; Bruce E. Steiner, "New England Anglicanism: A Genteel Faith?" *William and Mary Quarterly,* 3rd ser., 27 (1970): 122–35; and Joseph J. Ellis, III, "Anglicans in Connecticut, 1725–1750: The Conversion of the Mis-

sionaries," *New England Quarterly,* 44 (1971): 66–81. Whether Anglican work was directed primarily to the Indians or to nurture and propagation among the colonists remains a matter of scholarly debate.

21. December 20, 1767 letter from Andrew Eliot to Thomas Hollis, "Letters from Andrew Eliot to Thomas Hollis," pp. 417–18.

22. April 18, 1768 letter from Samuel Cooper to William Livingston, William Livingston Papers, Massachusetts Historical Society.

23. Charles Chauncy, *The Validity of Presbyterian Ordination Asserted and Maintained* (Boston: Richard Draper and Thomas Leverett, 1762). Also see the correspondence between Henry Caner and the Archbishop of Canterbury on this lecture in William S. Perry, ed., *Historical Collections Relating to the American Colonial Church,* 3 (New York: AMS Press, 1969), pp. 489, 495; and also Earl M. Wilbur, *A History of Unitarianism in Transylvania, England, and America* (Cambridge: Harvard University Press, 1952), p. 268.

24. *A Letter to a Friend, Containing Remarks on Certain Passages in a Sermon Preached by the Right Reverend Father in God, John Lord Bishop of Landaff* (Boston: Kneeland and Adams for Thomas Leverett, 1767), p. 26. It should be noted that Chauncy did not espouse liberty of conscience for everyone. If he did, he would have had to recognize the right of Roman Catholics to the same privileges he was defending. He endorsed such liberty only for his Puritan peers, although the pragmatic situation in his time had already decreed the necessity of concessions to Anglicans, Baptists, and Quakers.

25. Ibid., p. 47–51.

26. *An Appeal to the Public, in Behalf of the Church of England in America* (New York: James Parker, 1767), pp. 47–48.

27. Ibid., p. 79ff.

28. *The Appeal to the Public Answered, in Behalf of the Non-Episcopal Churches in America* (Boston: Kneeland and Adams for Thomas Leverett, 1768), pp. 56–58, 137, 144–51.

29. Ibid., pp. 192–205.

30. Ibid., p. 180.

31. *The Appeal Defended, or the Proposed American Episcopate Vindicated . . .* (New York: Hugh Gaines, 1769).

32. *A Reply to Dr. Chandler's "Appeal Defended"...* (Boston: Daniel Kneeland for Thomas Leverett, 1770), pp. 19–70.

33. Ibid., p. 103.

34. *The Appeal Farther Defended; in Answer to the Farther Misrepresentations of Dr. Chauncy* (New York: Hugh Gaines, 1771). In the absence of regulation church government, parish vestries in the colonies had exercised much more extensive power than that prescribed by normal practice. Some laity in positions of power therefore initially viewed the appointment of an American bishop as a demand that they yield the control over parish affairs they had come to cherish.

35. *A Compleat View of Episcopacy, as Exhibited from the Fathers of the Christian Church, until the Close of the Second Century* (Boston: Daniel Kneeland for Thomas Leverett, 1771).

36. Ibid., p. 72.

37. See the September 29, 1766 letter from Chauncy to Ezra Stiles, Stiles Papers, Yale University.

38. "Lettr. fro. Dissenters in London to Ministers in Massachusetts," *The Belknap Papers, 6 Collections* Massachusetts Historical Society, 4 (Boston: For the Society, 1891), pp. 23–25; March 30, 1767, May 29, 1767, and June 12, 1768, letters from Chauncy to Stiles and the May 28, 1772, letter from Stiles to Chauncy, Stiles Papers.

39. *Records of the General Association of the Clergy of Connecticut, 1738–1799,* ed. L. Perrin (Hartford: Press of the Case, Lockwood & Brainard Co., 1888), 63–64.

40. Chauncy's position was attacked in the May 9, May 23, July 4, August 8, September 12, September 19, November 21, November 28, and December 19, 1768, issues and the February 20 and March 13, 1769, issues of the *New York Gazette . . . Mercury,* and in the May 2, November 4, and November 28, 1768, issues and the February 13 and April 24, 1769, issues of the *New York Gazette . . . Post-Boy.*

41. Heimert, p. 361.

42. *Extracts from the Itineraries and Other Miscellanies of Ezra Stiles,* ed. Franklin B. Dexter (New Haven: Yale University Press, 1916), p. 450.

43. See the April 4 and April 25, 1768, letters from Chauncy to Stiles, Stiles Papers.

44. February 13, 1818, letter to Hezekiah Niles, *The Works of John Adams,* ed. Charles Francis Adams, 10 vols. (Boston: Little, Brown, 1850–1856), vol. 10, p. 288.

45. See Williston Walker, "The Sandemanians of New England,"

Annual Report of the American Historical Association for the Year 1901 (Washington: Government Printing Office, 1902), pp. 131–62.

46. November 10 and November 29, 1764, letters from Chauncy to Ezra Stiles, Stiles Papers.

47. *Twelve Sermons . . . with Interspersed Notes* (Boston: D. and J. Kneeland for Thomas Leverett, 1765).

48. Ibid., p. 339.

49. *Boston Gazette,* May 12, 1768.

50. Ernest Cassara, ed., *Universalism in America: A Documentary History* (Boston: Beacon Press, 1971), p. 13.

51. John Rowe, *Letters and Diary of John Rowe, Boston Merchant, 1759–1762, 1764–1779,* ed. Anne Rowe Cunningham (Boston: W.B. Clarke, 1903), p. 172; Hamilton A. Hill, *History of the Old South Church (Third Church) Boston, 1669–1884,* 2 vols. (Boston and New York: Houghton, Mifflin, 1890), vol. 2, p. 85.

52. *A Discourse Occasioned by the Death of the Reverned* [sic] *Jonathan Mayhew, D.D.* (Boston: Edes and Gill, 1766); *A Sermon Preached May 6, 1767. At the Ordination of the Rev. Simeon Howard, M.A.* (Boston: Edes and Gill, 1767).

53. February 17, 1766 Report of Committee to Assess Plagiarism Charge against Rev. Penuel Bowen for a Sermon on Eph. 4:8 Similar to Two Sermons by Dr. Doddridge, Miscellaneous Bound Mss., Massachusetts Historical Society; Hill, 2, p. 111.

54. *A Discourse Occasioned by the Death of the Reverend Dr. Joseph Sewall* (Boston: Kneeland and Adams, 1769); *A Discourse Occasioned by the Death of the Reverend Thomas Foxcroft, M.A.* (Boston: Daniel Kneeland for Thomas Leverett, 1769).

55. Robert F. Seybolt, "The Ministers at the Town Meeting in Colonial Boston," *Publications* Colonial Society of Massachusetts, 23 (Boston: Colonial Society of Massachusetts, 1937), p. 301; Boston Registry Department, *Records Relating to the Early History of Boston,* 20: *A Report of the Record Commissioners of the City of Boston, Containing the Selectmen's Minutes from 1764 through 1768* (Boston: Rockwell and Churchill, 1889), p. 299; Rowe, p. 172.

CHAPTER 5

1. See Oliver M. Dickerson, "Writs of Assistance as a Cause of the Revolution," in *The Era of the American Revolution,* ed. Richard B. Morris (New York: Columbia University Press, 1939), pp. 40–75.

2. The text of Otis's inflammatory address was not published at the time. An account of the event may be found in William Tudor, *The Life of James Otis* (Boston: Wells and Lilly, 1823), pp. 56ff. Also see Joseph R. Frese, "James Otis and Writs of Assistance," *New England Quarterly,* 30 (1957): 496–508; and John J. Waters and John A. Schutz, "Patterns of Massachusetts Colonial Politics: The Writs of Assistance and the Rivalry between the Otis and Hutchinson Families," *William and Mary Quarterly,* 3rd ser., 24 (1967): 543–68.

3. See "Letter to the People of Pennsylvania, &c.," *Pamphlets of the American Revolution, 1750–1776,* 1, ed. Bernard Bailyn (Cambridge: Belknap Press of Harvard University, 1965), pp. 257–72; John Adams, "Thoughts on Government" (1776), in *The Political Writings of John Adams,* ed. George A. Peek, Jr. (Indianapolis: Bobbs-Merrill, 1954), p. 90.

4. See David S. Lovejoy, "Rights Imply Equality: The Case Against Vice-Admiralty Jurisdiction in America, 1764–1776," *William and Mary Quarterly,* 3rd ser., 16 (1959): 459–84; and Carl Ubbelohde, *The Vice-Admiralty Courts and the American Revolution* (Chapel Hill: University of North Carolina Press for the Institute of Early American History and Culture, 1960), pp. 128–47, 202–11.

5. See Oxenbridge Thacher, "The Sentiments of a British American" (1764), in *Pamphlets of the American Revolution,* 1, pp. 492–93, and the December 20, 1765, letter from Samuel Adams (for the Boston members of the General Court) to Dennys DeBerdt, *The Writings of Samuel Adams,* ed. Harry Alonzo Cushing, 4 vols. (New York: G.P. Putnam's Sons, 1904–1908), vol. 1, p. 65.

6. See *John Dickinson's Farmer's Letters* (Philadelphia: n.p., 1801), p. 45.

7. The *Boston Gazette,* November 2, 1772, presented one statement of this view.

8. October 5, 1772, letter from Charles Chauncy to Richard Price, "The Price Letters," 2 *Proceedings* Massachusetts Historical Society, 17 (Boston: For the Society, 1903), pp. 265–66. In "Trans-Atlantic Dissent and the Revolution: Richard Price and Charles Chauncy," *Eighteenth-Century Life,* 4:2 (1977): 31–37, I compare and contrast in more detail the interpretations of Revolutionary events articulated by Price and Chauncy.

9. John Shy, *Toward Lexington: The Role of the British Army in the*

Coming of the American Revolution (Princeton: Princeton University Press, 1965), pp. 45–83, offers a cogent analysis of the various elements in the decision to station a standing army in the colonies.

10. *The Votes and Proceedings of the Freeholders and Other Inhabitants of the Town of Boston* (Boston: Edes and Gill, [1772]), p. 18; November 7, 1768, letter from Chauncy to Ezra Stiles, Stiles Papers, Yale University.

11. *Farmer's Letters,* pp. 4–6.

12. *Peter Oliver's Origin and Progress of the American Revolution: A Tory View,* ed. Douglass Adair and John A. Schutz (San Marino, Calif.: Huntington Library, 1963), p. 92.

13. June 4, 1770, entry in *The Literary Diary of Ezra Stiles,* ed. Franklin B. Dexter, 3 vols. (New York: Charles Scribner's Sons, 1901), vol. 1, p. 54.

14. *Trust in God, the Duty of a People in a Day of Trouble* (Boston: Daniel Kneeland for Thomas Leverett, 1770).

15. March 18, 1772, entry in *The Literary Diary of Ezra Stiles,* 1, p. 218.

16. Timothy H. Breen has examined this theme in early American Puritan thought in his *The Character of the Good Ruler: Puritan Political Ideas in New England, 1630–1730* (New Haven: Yale University Press, 1970).

17. The corruption/conspiracy matrix is prominent, for example, in *A Ministerial Catechise, Suitable to Be Learned by All Modern Provincial Governors, Pensioners, Placemen, &c.* (Boston: Isaiah Thomas, 1771); Samuel Langdon's election sermon entitled *Government Corrupted by Vice and Recovered by Righteousness* (Boston: Benjamin Edes, 1775); and Mercy Otis Warren's highly biased *History of the Rise, Progress and Termination of the American Revolution,* 3 vols. (Boston: Manning & Loring for E. Larkin, 1805).

18. "Price Letters," p. 267. Also see Jack M. Sosin, "The Massachusetts Acts of 1774: Coercive or Preventive?" *Huntington Library Quarterly,* 26 (1962–63): 235–52.

19. Boston Registry Department, *Records Relating to the Early History of Boston,* 18: *A Report of the Record Commissioners of the City of Boston, Containing the Boston Town Records, 1770 through 1777* (Boston: Rockwell and Churchill, 1887), p. 183.

20. *A Letter to a Friend, Giving a Concise, but Just, Representation of the Hardships and Sufferings the Town of Boston Is Exposed to, and Must*

Undergo in Consequence of the British-Parliament (Boston: Greenleaf's Printing Office, 1774), pp. 16–17, 24–25.

21. Ibid., pp. 12–13.

22. "Price Letters," p. 269.

23. April 9, 1776, letter from Andrew Eliot to Isaac Smith, Smith-Carter Papers, Massachusetts Historical Society.

24. The original manuscript of the motion is in the Washburn Collection, Massachusetts Historical Society.

25. "Letter from the General Association of Congregational Ministers in Connecticut, to the Clergymen in Boston," 2 *Collections* Massachusetts Historical Society, 2 (Boston: John Eliot, 1814), pp. 255–56.

26. September 13, 1774, letter from Chauncy to Thomas Amory, Massachusetts Historical Society.

27. August 26, 1774, letter from Chauncy to Samuel Adams, Samuel Adams Papers, New York Public Library.

28. November 3 and November 4, 1774, letters from Chauncy to Josiah Quincy, Jr., Josiah Quincy Papers, Massachusetts Historical Society.

29. "Copy of a Royalist Handbill Distributed among the British Soldiers at Boston, September 1774," *New England Historical and Genealogical Register,* 21 (1887): 60.

30. July 1, 1774, entry in "Extracts from the Journal of Thomas Hutchinson, Governor of Massachusetts," 1 *Proceedings* Massachusetts Historical Society, 15 (Boston: For the Society, 1878), p. 5.

31. *Peter Oliver's Origin and Progress,* p. 101.

32. The most astute portrayal is Bernard Bailyn, *The Ordeal of Thomas Hutchinson* (Cambridge: Harvard University Press, 1974).

33. August 5, 1775, Report of Committee to Design New Seal for Massachusetts, Massachusetts General Court Records, photostat, Massachusetts Historical Society.

34. Chauncy's younger daughter, Sally, had become the third wife of Roxbury's anti-episcopacy and pro-independence pastor, Amos Adams, in 1771.

35. August 14, 1776, letter from Abigail Adams to John Adams, *Familiar Letters of John Adams and His Wife Abigail Adams, during the Revolution* (New York: Hurd and Houghton, 1875), pp. 211–12.

36. "Price Letters," p. 267.

37. Alan Heimert, *Religion and the American Mind: From the Great*

Awakening to the Revolution (Cambridge: Harvard University Press, 1966), p. 387.

38. *The Accursed Thing Must Be Taken Away from among a People, if They Would Reasonably Hope to Stand before Their Enemies* (Boston: Thomas and John Fleet, 1778), p. 6.

39. Ibid., p. 15.

40. Ibid., pp. 17–23.

41. Tory spokesmen, of course, believed that submission to British authority would restore the same patterns of liberty which Chauncy sought to defend through rebellion. See Daniel Leonard, *Massachusettensis: or a Series of Letters, Containing a Faithful State of Many Important and Striking Facts Which Laid the Foundation of the Present Trouble in the Province of the Massachusetts-Bay . . .* (London: Reprinted for J. Mathews, 1776), and [Samuel Seabury], *The Congress Canvassed: or, an Examination into the Conduct of the Delegates at Their Grand Convention, Held in Philadelphia, Sept. 1, 1774* ([New York]: James Rivington, 1774).

42. See Eric Voegelin, *The New Science of Politics* (Chicago: University of Chicago Press, 1952); and Willmoore Kendall and George W. Carey, *The Basic Symbols of the American Political Tradition* (Baton Rouge: Louisiana State University Press, 1970), chapters 1 and 2. For a complimentary, though not identical, view, see Bernard Bailyn, "The Central Themes of the American Revolution: An Interpretation," *Essays on the American Revolution,* ed. Stephen G. Kurtz and James W. Hutson (Chapel Hill: University of North Carolina Press for the Institute of Early American History and Culture, 1973), pp. 3–31.

43. July 18, 1775, letter from Chauncy to Richard Price, "Price Letters," p. 298.

CHAPTER 6

1. Robert F. Seybolt, "The Ministers at the Town Meeting in Colonial Boston," *Publications* Colonial Society of Massachusetts, 32 (Boston: Colonial Society of Massachusetts, 1937), p. 301; Barney L. Jones, "Charles Chauncy and the Great Awakening in New England" (unpublished Ph.D. dissertation, Duke University, 1958), p. 175.

2. John Hunt, *A Sermon Preached September 25th 1771 . . . To Which Is Added, the Charge by the Rev. Dr. Chauncy . . .* (Boston: Kneeland

and Adams, 1772); Hamilton A. Hill, *History of the Old South Church (Third Church) Boston, 1669–1884,* 2 vols. (Boston and New York: Houghton, Mifflin, 1890), vol. 2, p. 150.

3. *The Result of an Ecclesiastical Council, Convened at Bolton, August 3, 1773* (Boston: Thomas and John Fleet, 1773).

4. Quoted in Aaron Bancroft, *A Sermon Delivered in Worcester, January 31, 1836* (Worcester: C. Harris, 1836), p. 36.

5. *Remarks on the Result of an Ecclesiastical Council, Which Met at Dorchester, on November 16, 1773* (Boston: John Boyle, 1774); *Sundry Votes Passed by the Church of Christ in Dorchester, Ann. Dom. 1773* (Boston: Mills and Hicks, 1774), pp. 3–4, 7–8, 15–21; Hill, 2, pp. 170–71.

6. March 19, 1777, letter from John Eliot to Jeremy Belknap, *The Belknap Papers, 6 Collections* Massachusetts Historical Society, 4 (Boston: For the Society, 1891), p. 107.

7. June 17, 1777, letter from John Eliot to Jeremy Belknap, ibid., pp. 123–24.

8. February 1781 letter from John Eliot to Jeremy Belknap, ibid., p. 207.

9. See Henry F. May, *The Enlightenment in America* (New York: Oxford University Press, 1976).

10. Quoted in Alden Bradford, *Memoirs of the Life and Writings of Rev. Jonathan Mayhew, D.D., Pastor of the West Church and Society in Boston, From June, 1747, to July, 1766* (Boston: C.C. Little & Co., 1838), p. 479.

11. July 31, 1779, letter from John Eliot to Jeremy Belknap, *Belknap Papers,* p. 145.

12. February 1781 letter from John Eliot to Jeremy Belknap, ibid., p. 207.

13. February 1, 1782, letter from John Eliot to Jeremy Belknap, ibid., pp. 225–26.

14. [Charles Chauncy], *Salvation for All Men, Illustrated and Vindicated as a Scripture Doctrine, in Numerous Extracts from a Variety of Pious and Learned Men, Who Have Purposely Writ upon the Subject* (Boston: T. and J. Fleet, 1782), p. iii.

15. *Belknap Papers,* pp. 236–37.

16. John Murray, *Letters and Sketches of Sermons,* 3 vols. (Boston: Joshua Belcher, 1812–13), vol. 2, p. 94.

17. The "pudding" was sent to London because of a shortage in

the United States of type for the numerous Greek words in the text.

18. Charles Chauncy, *The Mystery Hid from Ages and Generations Made Manifest by the Gospel-Revelation: or, the Salvation of All Men the Grand Thing Aimed at in the Scheme of God* (London: n.p., 1784), p. 1.

19. *Piety versus Moralism: The Passing of the New England Theology* (New York: H. Holt & Co., 1932), p. 145.

20. *The Benevolence of the Deity* (Boston: Powars & Willis, 1784), p. 74. Philip Greven, *The Protestant Temperament: Patterns of Child-Rearing, Religious Experience, and the Self in Early America* (New York: Alfred A. Knopf, 1977), relied heavily on this work to make his case that Chauncy represented a "moderate" position in seeing human happiness emerging largely from developing the ability to control the self, particularly the emotions.

21. *Benevolence,* p. 85.

22. Ibid., p. 97.

23. Ibid., p. 79.

24. Ibid., p. 193.

25. Ibid., pp. 174–203.

26. Ibid., p. 184.

27. Ibid., pp. 254–90.

28. *The Beginnings of Unitarianism in America* (Boston: Beacon Press, 1955), p. 183.

29. *Benevolence,* pp. 268–72.

30. Ibid., pp. 203–54.

31. Ibid., p. 213.

32. Ibid., p. 231.

33. *Five Dissertations on the Scripture Account of the Fall; and Its Consequences* (London: C. Dilly, 1785), pp. 191, 202–9.

34. Ibid., pp. 129–232, esp. pp. 152, 163–65, 171–72. Parts of the work are an attack on Jonathan Edwards, *Original Sin,* ed. Clyde A. Holbrook, *The Works of Jonathan Edwards,* 3 (New Haven: Yale University Press, 1970).

35. *Five Dissertations,* p. 131.

36. Ibid., pp. 132–33, 173–74.

37. Ibid., p. 58.

38. *Benevolence,* p. 167.

39. Romans 5:6–11. See Charles Chauncy, *Divine Glory Brought to View in the Final Salvation of All Men* (Boston: T. and J. Fleet, 1783), pp. 11–13.

40. *Benevolence,* p. 214; *Five Dissertations,* p. 40.

41. Alan Heimert, *Religion and the American Mind: From the Great Awakening to the Revolution* (Cambridge: Harvard University Press, 1966), p. 47; James W. Jones, *The Shattered Synthesis: New England Puritanism before the Great Awakening* (New Haven: Yale University Press, 1973), pp. 185, 189.

42. See Norman Pettit, *The Heart Prepared: Grace and Conversion in Puritan Spiritual Life* (New Haven: Yale University Press, 1966).

43. *Mystery Hid,* pp. 319–20.

44. Ibid., pp. 9, 11, 168, 238.

45. *Benevolence,* pp. 242–43.

46. *Mystery Hid,* p. 168.

47. Ibid., p. 85.

48. *Salvation for All Men,* pp. 8–9.

49. *Mystery Hid,* p. 219.

50. *Ten New England Leaders* (New York: Silver, Burdett and Co., 1901), p. 300.

51. May, pp. 56–58.

52. November 13, 1784, letter from Ebenezer Hazard to Jeremy Belknap, *The Belknap Papers,* 5 *Collections* Massachusetts Historical Society, 2 (Boston: For the Society, 1877), p. 406.

53. August 8, 1785, letter from John Jackson to Richard Price, "The Price Letters," 2 *Proceedings* Massachusetts Historical Society, 17 (Boston: For the Society, 1903), p. 330.

54. *Records of the First Church in Boston, Publications* Colonial Society of Massachusetts, 40 (Boston: Colonial Society of Massachusetts, 1961), pp. 573–74. Also see *The Literary Diary of Ezra Stiles,* ed. Franklin B. Dexter, 3 vols. (New York: Charles Scribner's Sons, 1901), vol. 3, p. 162.

55. February 24, 1785, letter from John Eliot to Jeremy Belknap, *Belknap Papers,* 6 *Collections* Massachusetts Historical Society, 4, p. 287.

CHAPTER 7

1. See the May 23, 1780, letter from John Eliot to Jeremy Belknap, *The Belknap Papers,* 6 *Collections* Massachusetts Historical Society, 4 (Boston: For the Society, 1891), p. 188. Backus castigated Chauncy's views in an article in the December 14, 1778, issue of the *Boston Gazette* and in his *Government and Liberty Described,* in *Isaac*

Backus on Church, State, and Calvinism, ed. William G. McLoughlin (Cambridge: Belknap Press of Harvard University, 1968), pp. 350–65. Also see Charles H. Lippy, "The 1780 Massachusetts Constitution: Religious Establishment or Civil Religion?" *Journal of Church and State,* 20 (1978): 533–49.

2. Edmund S. Morgan, *The Gentle Puritan: A Life of Ezra Stiles, 1727–1795* (New Haven: Yale University Press, 1962), p. 380.

3. *Memoirs of the American Academy of Arts and Sciences,* 1 (Boston: Adams and Nourse, 1785), appendix to Charter, 1.

4. "List of Portraits in the Hall of the Historical Society," 2 *Collections* Massachusetts Historical Society, 10 (Boston: For the Society, 1838), p. 290.

5. John Clarke, *A Discourse, Delivered at the First Church in Boston, February 15, 1787, at the Interment of the Rev. Charles Chauncy, D.D. A.A.S., Its Senior Pastor, Who Expired, Feb. 10, 1787* (Boston: James D. Griffith and Edward E. Powars, 1787).

6. Bezaleel Howard in *Annals of the American Pulpit,* 8, ed. William B. Sprague (New York: P. Carter, 1865), p. 13.

7. William H. Sumner, *History of East Boston* (Boston: J.E. Tilton & Co., 1858), pp. 264–65.

8. June 3, 1760, entry, Ebenezer Parkman Diary, American Antiquarian Society.

9. Comment dated February 1, 1760, Wheelock Mss., Dartmouth College Archives.

10. *Peter Oliver's Origin and Progress of the American Revolution: A Tory View,* ed. Douglass Adair and John A. Schutz (San Marino, Calif.: Huntington Library, 1963), p. 43.

Selected Bibliography

THE WRITINGS OF CHARLES CHAUNCY

The Accursed Thing Must Be Taken Away from among a People, if They Would Reasonably Hope to Stand before Their Enemies. Boston: Thomas and John Fleet, 1778.

All Nations of the Earth Blessed in Christ, the Seed of Abraham. Boston: John Draper, 1762.

The Appeal to the Public Answered, in Behalf of the Non-Episcopal Churches in America. Boston: Kneeland and Adams for Thomas Leverett, 1768.

The Benevolence of the Deity. Boston: Powars and Willis, 1784.

The Blessedness of the Dead Who Die in the Lord. Boston: Rogers and Fowle, 1749.

"Breaking of Bread," in Remembrance of the Dying Love of Christ, a Gospel Institution. Boston: Printed for Thomas Leverett, 1772.

The Character and Overthrow of Laish Considered and Applied. Boston: S. Kneeland and T. Green for D. Henchman, 1734.

Charity to the Distressed Members of Christ Accepted as Done to Himself, and Rewarded, at the Judgment-Day, with Blessedness in God's Everlasting Kingdom. Boston: Green and Russell, 1757.

Christian Love, as Exemplified by the First Christian Church in Their Having all Things in Common, Placed in Its True and Just Point of Light. Boston: Thomas Leverett, 1773.

Civil Magistrates Must Be Just, Ruling in the Fear of God. Boston: Printed by order of the Honourable House of Representatives, 1747.

A Compleat View of Episcopacy, as Exhibited from the Fathers of the Christian Church, until the Close of the Second Century. Boston: Daniel Kneeland for Thomas Leverett, 1771.

Cornelius's Character. Boston: D. Gookin, 1745.

The Counsel of Two Confederate Kings to Set the Son of Tabeal on the Throne, Represented as Evil, in It's Natural Tendency and Moral Aspect. Boston: D. Gookin, 1746.

A Discourse Occasioned by the Death of the Reverend Dr. Joseph Sewall, Late Colleague Pastor of the South-Church in Boston. Boston: Kneeland and Adams, 1769.

A Discourse Occasioned by the Death of the Reverned [sic] *Jonathan Mayhew, D.D., Late Pastor of the West-Church in Boston.* Boston: Edes and Gill, 1766.

A Discourse Occasioned by the Death of the Reverend Thomas Foxcroft, M.A., Late Colleague-Pastor of the First Church of Christ in Boston. Boston: Daniel Kneeland for Thomas Leverett, 1769.

A Discourse on "the Good News from a Far Country." Boston: Kneeland and Adams for Thomas Leverett, 1766.

Divine Glory Brought to View in the Final Salvation of All Men. Boston: T. and J. Fleet, 1783.

The Duty of Ministers to "Make Known the Mystery of the Gospel;" and the Duty of People to "Pray for Them," that They May Do It "with Boldness," or Fortitude. Boston: Edes and Gill, 1766.

Early Piety Recommended and Exemplified. Boston: S. Kneeland and T. Green for B. Gray, 1732.

The Earth Delivered from the Curse to Which It Is, at Present, Subjected. Boston: Edes and Gill, 1756.

Earthquakes a Token of the Righteous Anger of God. Boston: Edes and Gill, 1755.

Enthusiasm Described and Caution'd Against. Boston: J. Draper for S. Eliot and J. Blanchard, 1742.

Five Dissertations on the Scripture Account of the Fall; and Its Consequences. London: C. Dilly, 1785.

The Gifts of the Spirit to Ministers Consider'd in Their Diversity. Boston: Rogers and Fowle, 1742.

The Horrid Nature, and Enormous Guilt of Murder. Boston: Thomas Fleet, 1754.

The Idle-Poor Secluded from the Bread of Charity by the Christian Law. Boston: Thomas Fleet, 1752.

Joy, the Duty of Survivors, on the Death of Pious Friends and Relatives. Boston: S. Kneeland and T. Green, 1741.

The Late Religious Commotions in New-England Considered. Boston: Green, Bushell, and Allen for T. Fleet, 1743. Published anonymously.

A Letter from a Gentleman in Boston to Mr. George Wishart, One of the Ministers of Edinburgh, Concerning the State of Religion in New-England. Edinburgh: Publisher's name cropped, 1742.

A Letter to a Friend, Containing Remarks on Certain Passages in a Sermon Preached by the Right Reverend Father in God, John Lord Bishop of Landaff. . . . Boston: Kneeland and Adams for Thomas Leverett, 1767.

A Letter to a Friend; Giving a Concise, but Just Account, According to the Advice Hitherto Received, of the Ohio-Defeat. Boston: Edes and Gill, 1755.

A Letter to a Friend. Giving a Concise, but Just, Representation of the Hardships and Sufferings the Town of Boston Is Exposed to, and Must Undergo in Consequence of the Late Act of the British-Parliament. Boston: Greenleaf's Printing Office, 1774. Published anonymously.

A Letter to the Reverend Mr. George Whitefield, Publickly Calling upon Him to Vindicate His Conduct, or Confess His Faults. Boston: T. Fleet, 1743.

A Letter to the Reverend Mr. George Whitefield, Vindicating Certain Passages He Has Excepted against, in a Late Book Entitled Seasonable Thoughts. . . . Boston: Rogers and Fowle for S. Eliot, 1745.

Letter to Thomas Prince. January 15, 1733. Massachusetts Historical Society.

"Life of the Rev. President (Charles) Chauncy, Written at the Request of Dr. Stiles, May 23, 1768." 1 *Collections* Massachusetts Historical Society, 10. Boston: Munroe, Francis & Parker, 1809. Pp. 171–80.

Man's Life Considered under the Similitude of Vapour, That Appeareth for a Little Time, and Then Vanisheth Away. Boston: B. Green, 1731.

"Marvellous Things Done by the Right Hand and Holy Arm of God in Getting Him the Victory". Boston: T. Fleet, 1745.

Ministers Cautioned against the Occasions of Contempt. Boston: Rogers and Fowle for Samuel Eliot, 1744.

Ministers Exhorted and Encouraged to Take Heed of Themselves and To

Their Doctrine. Boston: Rogers and Fowle for S. Eliot, 1744.

The Mystery Hid from Ages and Generations Made Manifest by the Gospel-Revelation: or, the Salvation of All Men the Grand Thing Aimed at in the Scheme of God. London: n.p., 1784.

Nathanael's Character Display'd. Boston: n.p., 1733.

The New Creature Describ'd, and Consider'd as the Sure Characteristick of a Man's Being in Christ. Boston: G. Rogers for J. Edwards and S. Eliot, 1741.

Notes on back flyleaf of Henry Flynt, *An Appeal to the Consciences, of a Degenerate People, for the Vindication of God's Proceedings with Them.* Boston: Printed for Samuel Gerrish. Copy of the Massachusetts Historical Society.

The Only Compulsion Proper to Be Made Use of in the Affairs of Conscience and Religion. Boston: J. Draper for J. Edwards, 1739.

The Opinion of One That Has Perused the Summer Morning's Conversation, Concerning Original Sin, Wrote by the Rev. Mr. Peter Clark. Boston: Green & Russell, 1758.

The Out-Pouring of the Holy Ghost. Boston: T. Fleet for D. Henchman and S. Eliot, 1742.

Prayer for Help a Seasonable Duty upon the Ceasing of Godly and Faithful Men. Boston: T. Fleet, 1737.

A Reply to Dr. Chandler's "Appeal Defended." . . . Boston: Daniel Kneeland for Thomas Leverett, 1770.

Salvation for All Men, Illustrated and Vindicated as a Scripture Doctrine, in Numerous Extracts from a Variety of Pious and Learned Men, Who Have Purposely Writ Upon the Subject. Boston: T. and J. Fleet, 1782. Published anonymously.

Seasonable Thoughts on the State of Religion in New-England, a Treatise in Five Parts. Boston: Rogers and Fowle for Samuel Eliot, 1743.

A Second Letter to a Friend; Giving a More Particular Narrative of the Defeat of the French Army at Lake George, by the New-England Troops, than Has Yet Been Published. Boston: Edes and Gill, 1755.

A Second Letter to the Reverend Mr. George Whitefield, Urging upon Him the Duty of Repentance, and Returning into the Bosom of That Church of Which He Professes Himself a Member and Minister. Boston: T. Fleet, 1745.

A Sermon Delivered at the First Church in Boston, March 13th, 1785:

Occasioned by the Return of the Society to Their House of Worship. . . . Boston: Greenleaf and Freeman, 1785.

A Sermon Preached May 6, 1767. At the Ordination of the Rev. Simeon Howard, M.A., to the Pastoral Care of the West-Church in Boston. Boston: Edes and Gill, 1767.

"A Sketch of Eminent Men in New-England." 1 *Collections* Massachusetts Historical Society, 10. Boston: Munroe, Francis & Parker, 1809. Pp. 154–70.

Trust in God, the Duty of a People in a Day of Trouble. Boston: Daniel Kneeland for Thomas Leverett, 1770.

Twelve Sermons . . . with Interspersed Notes. Boston: D. and J. Kneeland for Thomas Leverett, 1765.

An Unbridled Tongue a Sure Evidence, that Our Religion Is Hypocritical and Vain. Boston: Rogers and Fowle, 1741.

The Validity of Presbyterian Ordination Asserted and Maintained. Boston: Richard Draper and Thomas Leverett, 1762.

PUBLISHED PRIMARY SOURCES

An Account of the Rise, Progress and Consequences of the Land Bank; and the Silver Schemes in the Province of the Massachusetts-Bay. Boston: n.p., 1744.

Adams, John, and Abigail Adams. *Familiar Letters of John Adams and His Wife Abigail Adams, During the Revolution.* New York: Hurd and Houghton, 1875.

Adams, John. *The Political Writings of John Adams: Representative Selections.* George A. Peek, Jr., ed. Indianapolis: Bobbs-Merrill, 1954.

Adams, John. *The Works of John Adams.* 10 vols. Charles Francis Adams, ed. Boston: Little, Brown, 1850–1856.

Adams, Samuel. *The Writings of Samuel Adams.* 4 vols. Harry Alonzo Cushing, ed. New York: G. P. Putnam's Sons, 1904–1908.

Backus, Isaac. *Isaac Backus on Church, State, and Calvinism: Pamphlets, 1754–1789.* William G. McLoughlin, ed. Cambridge: Belknap Press of Harvard University, 1968.

Bailyn, Bernard, ed. *Pamphlets of the American Revolution, 1750–1776.* Vol. 1: 1750–1765. Cambridge: Belknap Press of Harvard University, 1965.

Bancroft, Aaron. *A Sermon Delivered in Worcester, January 31, 1836.* Worcester: C. Harris, 1836.

The Belknap Papers. 5 *Collections* Massachusetts Historical Society, 2. Boston: For the Society, 1877.

The Belknap Papers. 6 *Collections* Massachusetts Historical Society, 4. Boston: For the Society, 1891.

[Bernard, Sir Francis]. *Letters to the Ministry from Governor Bernard, General Gage, and Commodore Hood.* Salem: Samuel Hall, 1769.

Boston Registry Department. *Records Related to the Early History of Boston.* Vol. 15: *A Report of the Record Commissioners of the City of Boston, Containing the Records of Boston Selectmen, 1736 to 1742;* Vol. 17: *A Report of the Record Commissioners of the City of Boston, Containing the Selectmen's Minutes from 1742–1743 to 1753;* Vol. 18: *A Report of the Record Commissioners of the City of Boston, Containing the Boston Town Records, 1770 through 1777;* Vol. 19: *A Report of the Record Commissioners of the City of Boston, Containing the Selectmen's Minutes from 1754 through 1763;* Vol. 20: *A Report of the Record Commissioners of the City of Boston, Containing the Selectmen's Minutes from 1764 through 1768;* Vol. 24: *A Report of the Record Commissioners of the City of Boston: Boston Births from 1700 to 1800.* Boston: Rockwell and Churchill, 1886–1894.

Cassara, Ernest, ed. *Universalism in America: A Documentary History.* Boston: Beacon Press, 1971.

Chandler, Thomas Bradbury. *The Appeal Defended, or the Proposed American Episcopate Vindicated. . . .* New York: Hugh Gaines, 1769.

Chandler, Thomas Bradbury. *The Appeal Farther Defended; in Answer to the Farther Misrepresentations of Dr. Chauncy.* New York: Hugh Gaines, 1771.

Chandler, Thomas Bradbury. *An Appeal to the Public, in Behalf of the Church of England in America.* New York: James Parker, 1767.

Chandler, Thomas Bradbury. *A Friendly Address to All Reasonable Americans, on the Subject of Our Political Confusions.* New York: James Rivington, 1774.

Chauncey, Charles. *God's Mercy, Shewed to His People in Giving Them a Faithful Ministry and Schools of Learning. . . .* Cambridge: Samuel Green, 1655.

Checkley, Samuel. "Diary of the Rev. Samuel Checkley, 1735." *Publications* Colonial Society of Massachusetts, 12. Boston: Colonial Society of Massachusetts, 1911. Pp. 270–306.

Clark, Peter. *Remarks on a Late Pamphlet intitled* [sic] *"The Opinion of*

One That Has Perused the Summer-Morning's Conversation Concerning the Doctrine of Original Sin." Boston: Edes and Gill, 1758.

Clark, Peter. *The Scripture-Doctrine of Original Sin, Stated and Defended. In a Summer-Morning's Conversation.* Boston: S. Kneeland, 1758.

Clarke, John. *A Discourse, Delivered at the First Church in Boston, February 15, 1787. at the Interment of the Rev. Charles Chauncy, D.D. A.A.S. Its Senior Pastor. . . .* Boston: James D. Griffith and Edward E. Powars, 1787.

Cooper, Samuel. "Diary of Rev. Samuel Cooper of Boston (1753–Jan. 1754)." *New England Historical and Genealogical Register,* 40 (1887): 388–91.

Cooper, Samuel. "Diary of Samuel Cooper, 1775–1776," ed. Frederick Tuckerman. *American Historical Review,* 6 (1901): 301–41.

"Copy of a Royalist Handbill distributed among the British Soldiers at Boston, September, 1774." *New England Historical and Genealogical Register,* 21 (1867): 60.

"Correspondence between Rev. Thomas Prince and Rev. Charles Chauncy," 4 *Collections* Massachusetts Historical Society, 4. Boston: For the Society, 1854. Pp. 238–39.

Davenport, James. *The Reverend Mr. James Davenport's Confession and Retractions.* Boston: S. Kneeland and T. Green, 1744.

Dickinson, John. *John Dickinson's Farmer's Letters.* Philadelphia: n.p., 1801.

Eckley, Joseph. *Divine Glory, Brought to View in the Condemnation of the Ungodly.* Boston: Robert Hodge, 1782.

Edwards, Jonathan. *The Distinguishing Marks of a Work of the Spirit of God.* Reprinted, London: S. Mason, 1742.

Edwards, Jonathan. *The Great Awakening.* C. C. Goen, ed. *The Works of Jonathan Edwards,* 4. New Haven and London: Yale University Press, 1972.

Edwards, Jonathan. *Original Sin.* Clyde A. Holbrook, ed. *The Works of Jonathan Edwards,* 3. New Haven: Yale University Press, 1970.

Edwards, Jonathan. *A Treatise Concerning Religious Affections.* John E. Smith, ed. *The Works of Jonathan Edwards,* 2. New Haven: Yale University Press, 1959.

Edwards, Jonathan. *Treatise on Grace and Other Posthumous Writings.* Paul Helm, ed. Cambridge and London: James Clarke & Co., 1971.

Edwards, Jonathan, Jr. *The Salvation of All Men Strictly Examined.* New Haven: A. Morse, 1790.

Eliot, Andrew. "Letters from Andrew Eliot to Thomas Hollis," 4 *Collections* Massachusetts Historical Society, 4. Boston: For the Society, 1858. Pp. 398–461.

Emerson, Joseph. *A Thanksgiving Sermon Preach'd at Pepperell, July 24th. 1766.* Boston: Edes and Gill, 1766.

General Association of the Clergy of Connecticut. *Records of the General Association of the Clergy of Connecticut, 1738–1799.* L. Perrin, ed. Hartford: Press of the Case, Lockwood & Brainard Co., 1888.

Gordon, William. *The Doctrine of Final Universal Salvation Examined and Shewn to Be Unscriptural.* Boston: T. and J. Fleet, 1783.

Hawley, Gideon. "A Letter from Rev. Gideon Hawley of Marshpec Containing a Narrative of His Journey to Onohoghwage in July, 1753." *Ecclesiastical Records, State of New York,* 5. E. T. Corwin, ed. Albany: J. B. Lyon, 1901.

Hopkins, Samuel. *Inquiry Concering* [sic] *the Future State of Those Who Die in Their Sins.* Newport: Solomon Southwick, 1783.

Hunt, John. *A Sermon Preached September 25th 1771 . . . To Which Is Added, the Charge by the Rev. Dr. Chauncy. . . .* Boston: Kneeland and Adams, 1772.

Hutchinson, Thomas. "Extracts from the Journal of Thomas Hutchinson, Governor of Massachusetts." 1 *Proceedings* Massachusetts Historical Society, 15. Boston: For the Society, 1878. Pp. 326–34.

[Ingersoll, Jared]. *Mr. Ingersoll's Letters Relating to the Stamp-Act.* New Haven: Samuel Green, 1766.

Langdon, Samuel. *Government Corrupted by Vice, and Recovered by Righteousness.* Watertown, Mass.: Benjamin Edes, 1775.

[Lee, Charles]. "Strictures on a Pamphlet, Entitled, a 'Friendly Address to All Reasonable Americans on the Subject of Our Political Confusions' " (1774). *Collections* New York Historical Society, 4. New York: Printed for the Society, 1872. Pp. 151–56.

Leonard, Daniel. *Massachusettensis: or a Series of Letters Containing a Faithful State of Many Important and Striking Facts Which Laid the Foundation of the Present Trouble in the Province of the Massachusetts-Bay. . . .* London: Reprinted for J. Mathews, 1776.

"Letter from the General Association of Congregational Ministers in Connecticut, to the Clergymen in Boston." 2 *Collections* Massachusetts Historical Society, 2. Boston: John Eliot, 1814. Pp. 255–56.

"Letters of Dr. Watts." 2 *Proceedings* Massachusetts Historical Society, 9. Boston: For the Society, 1895. Pp. 331–410.

Mather, Cotton. *Magnalia Christi Americana.* 2 vols. Hartford: Published by Silas Andrus, 1820.

Mather, Samuel. *All Men Will Not Be Saved Forever.* Boston: Benjamin Edes & Sons, 1782.

Mayhew, Jonathan. *A Discourse Concerning Unlimited Submission and Non-Resistance to the Higher Powers.* Boston: D. Fowle and D. Gookin, 1750.

Mayhew, Jonathan. *A Sermon Preach'd in the Audience of His Excellence William Shirley. . . .* Boston: Samuel Kneeland, 1754.

Mayhew, Jonathan. *Seven Sermons.* Boston: Rogers and Fowle, 1749.

Mayhew, Jonathan. *The Snare Broken.* Boston: Edes and Gill, 1766.

Mayhew, Jonathan. *Two Discourses Delivered November 23d. 1758.* Boston: Edes and Gill, 1758.

Memoirs of the American Academy of Arts and Sciences: to the End of the Year M, DCC, LXXXIII. Vol. 1. Boston: Adams and Nourse, 1785.

A Ministerial Catechise, Suitable to Be Learned by All Modern Provincial Governors, Pensioners, Placemen, &c.. Boston: Isaiah Thomas, 1771.

Murray, John. *Letters and Sketches of Sermons.* 3 vols. Boston: Joshua Belcher, 1812–1813.

Oliver, Peter. *Peter Oliver's Origin and Progress of the American Revolution: A Tory View.* Douglass Adair and John A. Schutz, eds. San Marino, Calif.: Huntington Library, 1963.

Osborn, Samuel. *The Case and Complaint of Mr. Samuel Osborn, Late of Eastham.* Boston: W. McAlpine, 1743.

Parkman, Ebenezer. *Journal of Ebenezer Parkman.* Westborough, Mass.: Privately printed, 1906.

The Pepperrell Papers. 6 *Collections* Massachusetts Historical Society, 10. Boston: For the Society, 1899.

Perry, William Stevens, ed. *Historical Collections Relating to the American Colonial Church.* Vol. 3. New York: AMS Press, 1969.

"The Price Letters." 2 *Proceedings* Massachusetts Historical Society, 17. Boston: For the Society, 1903. Pp. 263–378.

Prince, Thomas. "Diary of the Rev. Thomas Prince." *Publications* Colonial Society of Massachusetts, 19. Boston: Colonial Society of Massachusetts, 1918. Pp. 331–64.

The Records of the First Church in Boston, 1630–1868. Richard D. Pierce, ed. *Publications* Colonial Society of Massachusetts, 39–41. Boston: Colonial Society of Massachusetts, 1961.

Remarks on the Result of an Ecclesiastical Council, Which Met at Dorchester, on November 16, 1773. Boston: John Boyle, 1774.

The Result of an Ecclesiastical Council, Convened at Bolton, August 3, 1773. Boston: Thomas and John Fleet, 1773.

Rowe, John. *Letters and Diary of John Rowe, Boston Merchant, 1759–1762, 1764–1779.* Anne Rowe Cunningham, ed. Boston: W. B. Clarke, 1903.

[Seabury, Samuel]. *The Congress Canvassed: or, an Examination into the Conduct of the Delegates at Their Grand Convention, Held in Philadelphia, Sept. 1, 1774.* [New York: James Rivington], 1774.

Sewall, Samuel. "Address in Opposition to Issuing More Paper Money," *Letter-Book of Samuel Sewall. 6 Collections* Massachusetts Historical Society, 2. Boston: For the Society, 1888. Pp. 235–39.

Sewall, Samuel. *Diary of Samuel Sewall. 5 Collections* Massachusetts Historical Society, 5–7. Boston: For the Society, 1878–1882.

A Short Narrative of the Horrid Massacre in Boston, Perpetrated in the Evening of the Fifth Day of March, 1770. . . . Freeport, N.Y.: Books for Libraries Press, 1971.

Sprague, William B., ed. *Annals of the American Pulpit.* Vol. 8. New York: P. Carter, 1865.

Stebbins, Rufus. *A Centennial Discourse Delivered to the First Congregational Church and Society in Leominster, September 24, 1843.* Boston: C. C. Little and J. Brown, 1843.

Stiles, Ezra. *Extracts from the Itineraries and Other Miscellanies of Ezra Stiles, D.D., LL.D., 1755–1794, with a Selection of His Correspondence.* Franklin B. Dexter, ed. New Haven: Yale University Press, 1916.

Stiles, Ezra. *The Literary Diary of Ezra Stiles.* Franklin B. Dexter, ed. 3 vols. New York: Charles Scribner's Sons, 1901.

Sundry Votes Passed by the Church of Christ in Dorchester Ann. Dom. 1773. Boston: Mills and Hicks, 1774.

Taylor, John. *The Scripture Doctrine of Original Sin, Proposed to a Free and Candid Examination.* London: Printed for the Author by J. Wilson, 1740.

Thacher, Peter. *That the Punishment of the Finally Impenitent Shall Be Eternal.* Salem: Samuel Hall, 1783.

Tennent, Gilbert. *The Danger of an Unconverted Ministry, Considered in a Sermon on Mark VI, 34.* Philadelphia: Benjamin Franklin, 1740.

The Votes and Proceedings of the Freeholders and Other Inhabitants of the Town of Boston. Boston: Edes and Gill, [1772].

Warren, Mercy Otis. *History of the Rise, Progress and Termination of the American Revolution, Interspersed with Biographical, Political and Moral Observations.* 3 vols. Boston: Manning & Loring for E. Larkin, 1805.

Webster, Samuel. *A Winter Evening's Conversation upon the Doctrine of Original Sin.* New Haven: Printed by James Parker, 1757.

Whitefield, George. *A Letter to the Reverend Dr. Chauncy, on Account of Some Passages Relating to the Revd. Mr. Whitefield in His Book Intitled* [sic] *Seasonable Thoughts. . . .* Boston: S. Kneeland and T. Green, 1745.

UNPUBLISHED PRIMARY SOURCES

Chauncy, Charles. Deed to William Pepperrell, April 21,1733. Massachusetts Historical Society.

Cooper, Samuel. April 18, 1768 letter to William Livingston. William Livingston Papers. Massachusetts Historical Society.

Cutler, Timothy. November 8, 1734 letter to Zachary Gray. Emmet Collection. New York Public Library.

Eliot, Andrew. April 9, 1776 letter to Isaac Smith. Smith-Carter Papers. Massachusetts Historical Society.

Eliot, Andrew. Ms. Diary of Andrew Eliot. Massachusetts Historical Society.

Harvard College. College Papers. Harvard University Archives.

Harvard College Faculty. Faculty Records. Harvard University Archives.

Motion by Charles Chauncy to Have Boston Clergy Cease Reading Government Proclamations in Meetinghouses. Washburn Collection. Massachusetts Historical Society.

Parkman, Ebenezer. Ebenezer Parkman Diary. American Antiquarian Society.

Penny, Timothy, and I. Gardiner. Report of Committee to Arbitrate Charles Chauncy's Claim to One-Third Interest in Antigua Sugar Plantation Held by His Late Wife. Greenough Papers. Massachusetts Historical Society.

Report of Committee to Assess Plagiarism Charge against Rev. Penuel Bowen for a Sermon on Ephesians 4:8 Similar to Two Sermons by Dr. Doddridge. Miscellaneous Bound Mss. Massachusetts Historical Society.

Report of Committee to Design New Seal for Massachusetts. Massachusetts General Court Records. Photostat, Massachusetts Historical Society.

Stiles, Ezra. Ezra Stiles Papers. Yale University.

Stiles, Ezra. March 19, 1770 letter to Charles Chauncy. Andrews-Eliot Papers. Massachusetts Historical Society.

Subscription for Support of Josiah Cotton (H.C. 1722) in Ministry at Providence, Rhode-Island. Colman Papers. Massachusetts Historical Society.

Wheelock, Eleazer. Wheelock Mss. Dartmouth College Archives.

NEWSPAPERS

Boston Gazette. Issues of November 2, 1772, and December 14, 1778.

Boston Weekly News-Letter. Issue of September 25, 1740.

New England Weekly Journal. Issue of January 23, 1739.

New York Gazette . . . Mercury. Issues of May 9, May 23, July 4, August 8, September 12, September 19, November 21, November 28, and December 19, 1768; and February 20 and March 13, 1769.

New York Gazette . . . Post-Boy. Issues of May 2, November 4, and November 28, 1768; and February 13 and April 24, 1769.

PUBLISHED SECONDARY SOURCES: ARTICLES AND ESSAYS

Bailyn, Bernard. "The Central Themes of the American Revolution." *Essays on the American Revolution.* Stephen G. Kurtz and James W. Hutson, eds. Chapel Hill: University of North Carolina Press for the Institute of Early American History and Culture, 1973. Pp. 3–31.

Dickerson, Oliver M. "Writs of Assistance as a Cause of the Revolution." *The Era of the American Revolution.* Richard B. Morris, ed.

New York: Columbia University Press, 1939. Pp. 40–75.

Ellis, Joseph J., III. "Anglicans in Connecticut, 1725–1750: The Conversion of the Missionaries." *New England Quarterly,* 44 (1971): 66–81.

Fowler, William C. "President Charles Chauncy and His Ancestors and Descendants." *New England Historical and Genealogical Register,* 10 (1856): 324–36.

Frese, Joseph R. "James Otis and Writs of Assistance." *New England Quarterly,* 30 (1957): 496–508.

Gaustad, Edwin S. "Charles Chauncy and the Great Awakening: A Survey and Bibliography." *The Papers of the Bibliographical Society of America,* 45 (1951): 125–35.

Gillett, E. H. "President Wheelock and Dr. Chauncy." *American Presbyterian Review,* 3rd ser., 11 (1871): 463–75.

Lane, William C. "New Hampshire's Part in Restoring the Library and Apparatus of Harvard College after the Fire of 1764." *Publications* Colonial Society of Massachusetts, 25. Boston: Colonial Society of Massachusetts, 1924. Pp. 24–33.

Lippy, Charles H. "The Great Awakening: An Opponent's Perspective." *Ohio Journal of Religious Studies,* 2:1 (1974): 44–52.

Lippy, Charles H. "Restoring a Lost Ideal: Charles Chauncy and the American Revolution." *Religion in Life,* 44 (1975): 491–502.

Lippy, Charles H. "The 1780 Massachusetts Constitution: Religious Establishment or Civil Religion?" *Journal of Church and State,* 20 (1978): 533–49.

Lippy, Charles H. "Trans-Atlantic Dissent and the Revolution: Richard Price and Charles Chauncy." *Eighteenth-Century Life,* 4:2 (1977): 31–37.

"List of Portraits in the Hall of the Historical Society." 2 *Collections* Massachusetts Historical Society, 10. Boston: For the Society, 1838. Pp. 285–91.

Lovejoy, David S. "Rights Imply Equality: The Case Against Admiralty Jurisdiction in America, 1764–1776." *William and Mary Quarterly,* 3rd ser., 16 (1959): 459–84.

Miller, John C. "Religion, Finance, and Democracy in Massachusetts." *New England Quarterly,* 6 (1933): 29–58.

Miller, Perry. "Jonathan Edwards and the Great Awakening." *Errand Into the Wilderness.* Cambridge: Harvard University Press, 1956. Pp. 153–66.

Mills, Frederick V. "Anglican Expansion in Colonial America, 1761–1775." *Historical Magazine of the Protestant Episcopal Church,* 39 (1970): 315–24.

Phillips, Ulrich B. "An Antigua Plantation, 1769–1818." *North Carolina Historical Review,* 3 (1926): 439–45.

Richey, McMurry S. "Jonathan Mayhew: American Christian Rationalist." *A Miscellany of American Christianity.* Stuart C. Henry, ed. Durham: Duke University Press, 1963. Pp. 292–327.

Seybolt, Robert F. "The Ministers at the Town Meetings in Colonial Boston." *Publications* Colonial Society of Massachusetts, 32. Boston: Colonial Society of Massachusetts, 1937. Pp. 300–304.

Sosin, Jack M. "The Massachusetts Acts of 1774: Coercive or Preventive?" *Huntington Library Quarterly,* 26 (1962–1963): 235–52.

Steiner, Bruce E. "New England Anglicanism: A Genteel Faith?" *William and Mary Quarterly,* 3rd ser., 27 (1970): 122–35.

Walker, Williston. "The Sandemanians of New England." *Annual Report of the American Historical Association for the Year 1901.* Washington: Government Printing Office, 1902. Pp. 131–62.

Waters, John J., and John A. Schutz. "Patterns of Massachusetts Colonial Politics: The Writs of Assistance and the Rivalry Between the Otis and Hutchinson Families." *William and Mary Quarterly,* 3rd ser., 24 (1967): 543–68.

PUBLISHED SECONDARY SOURCES: BOOKS

Akers, Charles W. *Called Unto Liberty: A Life of Jonathan Mayhew, 1720–1766.* Cambridge: Harvard University Press, 1964.

Albanese, Catherine L. *Sons of the Fathers: The Civil Religion of the American Revolution.* Philadelphia: Temple University Press, 1976.

Bailyn, Bernard. *Ideological Origins of the American Revolution.* Cambridge: Harvard University Press, 1967.

Bailyn, Bernard. *The Ordeal of Thomas Hutchinson.* Cambridge: Harvard University Press, 1974.

Bailyn, Bernard. *The Origins of American Politics.* New York: Vintage Books, 1968.

Billias, George A. *The Massachusetts Land Bankers of 1740.* University of Maine Studies, 2nd ser., No. 74. Orono: University of Maine Press, 1959.

Bradford, Alden. *Memoir of the Life and Writings of Rev. Jonathan Mayhew, D.D., Pastor of the West Church and Society in Boston, From June, 1747, to July, 1766.* Boston: C.C. Little & Co., 1838.

Brauer, Jerald C., ed. *Religion and the American Revolution.* Philadelphia: Fortress Press, 1976.

Breen, Timothy H. *The Character of the Good Ruler: Puritan Political Ideas in New-England, 1630–1730.* New Haven: Yale University Press, 1970.

Bridenbaugh, Carl. *Cities in the Wilderness: Urban Life in America, 1625–1742.* New York: Capricorn Books, 1964; first pub., 1938.

Bridenbaugh, Carl. *Mitre and Sceptre: Transatlantic Faiths, Ideas, Personalities, and Politics, 1689–1775.* New York: Oxford University Press, 1962.

Bushman, Richard L. *From Puritan to Yankee: Character and the Social Order in Connecticut, 1690–1765.* Cambridge: Harvard University Press, 1967.

Cross, Arthur L. *The Anglican Episcopate and the American Colonies.* New York and London: Longmans, Green and Co., 1902.

Delattre, Roland A. *Beauty and Sensibility in the Thought of Jonathan Edwards.* New Haven: Yale University Press, 1970.

Demos, John. *A Little Commonwealth: Family Life in Plymouth Colony.* London and New York: Oxford University Press, 1970.

Ford, Paul L. *Bibliotheca Chaunciana: A List of the Writings of Charles Chauncy.* Elzevir Club Series, No. 6. Brooklyn: Privately printed, 1884.

Gaustad, Edwin S. *The Great Awakening in New England.* New York: Harper and Row, 1957.

Goen, C.C. *Revivalism and Separatism in New England, 1740–1800: Strict Congregationalists and Separate Baptists in the Great Awakening.* New Haven: Yale University Press, 1962.

Greene, Jack P., ed. *The Reinterpretation of the American Revolution, 1763–1789.* New York: Harper and Row, 1968.

Greven, Philip. *The Protestant Temperament: Patterns of Child-Rearing, Religious Experience, and the Self in Early America.* New York: Alfred A. Knopf, 1977.

Haroutunian, Joseph. *Piety Versus Moralism: The Passing of the New England Theology.* New York: Henry Holt and Co., 1932.

Heimert, Alan. *Religion and the American Mind: From the Great Awak-*

ening to the Revolution. Cambridge: Harvard University Press, 1966.

Hill, Hamilton A. *History of the Old South Church (Third Church) Boston, 1669–1884.* 2 vols. Boston and New York: Houghton, Mifflin and Co., 1890.

Hudson, Winthrop S. *Religion in America.* New York: Charles Scribner's Sons, 1965.

Jennings, Francis. *The Invasion of America: Indians, Colonialism, and the Cant of Conquest.* Chapel Hill: University of North Carolina Press for the Institute of Early American History and Culture, 1975.

Jones, James W. *The Shattered Synthesis: New England Puritanism Before the Great Awakening.* New Haven: Yale University Press, 1973.

Kendall, Willmoore, and George W. Carey. *The Basic Symbols of the American Political Tradition.* Baton Rouge: Louisiana State University Press, 1970.

Koch, Gustav Adolf. *Republican Religion: The American Revolution and the Cult of Reason.* New York: Henry Holt and Co., 1933.

McGiffert, Arthur C., Jr. *Jonathan Edwards.* New York and London: Harper and Bros., 1932.

McLoughlin, William G. *New England Dissent, 1630–1833: The Baptists and the Separation of Church and State.* 2 vols. Cambridge: Harvard University Press, 1971.

May, Henry F. *The Enlightenment in America.* New York: Oxford University Press, 1976.

Miller, Perry. *Jonathan Edwards.* New York: W. Sloane Associates, 1949.

Morgan, Edmund S. *The Gentle Puritan: A Life of Ezra Stiles, 1727–1795.* New Haven: Yale University Press for the Institute of Early American History and Culture, 1962.

Morgan, Edmund S. *The Puritan Family.* Rev. ed. New York: Harper and Row, 1966.

Morgan, Edmund S. and Helen M. Morgan. *The Stamp Act Crisis: Prologue to Revolution.* Chapel Hill: University of North Carolina Press for the Institute of Early American History and Culture, 1953.

Niebuhr, H. Richard. *The Kingdom of God in America.* New York: Harper and Bros., 1937.

Parrington, Vernon L. *Main Currents in American Thought.* 3 vols. New York: Harcourt, Brace, and Co., 1927–1930.

Pettit, Norman. *The Heart Prepared: Grace and Conversion in Puritan Spiritual Life.* New Haven: Yale University Press, 1966.

Seybolt, Robert F. *The Public Schools of Colonial Boston, 1635–1775.* Cambridge: Harvard University Press, 1935.

Shipton, Clifford K. *Sibley's Harvard Graduates.* Vols. 6–8. Boston: For the Massachusetts Historical Society, 1942–1951.

Shy, John. *Toward Lexington: The Role of the British Army in the Coming of the American Revolution.* Princeton: Princeton University Press, 1965.

Slotkin, Richard. *Regeneration Through Violence: The Mythology of the American Frontier, 1600–1860.* Middletown, Conn.: Wesleyan University Press, 1973.

Sumner, William H. *History of East Boston.* Boston: J.E. Tilton & Co., 1858.

Tracy, Joseph. *The Great Awakening: A History of the Revival of Religion in the Time of Edwards and Whitefield.* Boston: Tappan and Sennet, 1842.

Tudor, William. *The Life of James Otis of Massachusetts.* Boston: Wells and Lilly, 1823.

Ubbelohde, Carl. *The Vice-Admiralty Courts and the American Revolution.* Chapel Hill: University of North Carolina Press for the Institute of Early American History and Culture, 1960.

Voegelin, Eric. *The New Science of Politics.* Chicago: University of Chicago Press, 1952.

Walker, Williston. *Ten New England Leaders.* New York and Boston: Silver, Burdett and Co., 1901.

Wilbur, Earl M. *A History of Unitarianism in Transylvania, England, and America.* Cambridge: Harvard University Press, 1952.

Wright, Conrad. *The Beginnings of Unitarianism in America.* Boston: Beacon Press, 1955.

Ziff, Larzer. *Puritanism in America: New Culture in a New World.* New York: Viking Press, 1973.

UNPUBLISHED SECONDARY SOURCES

Bernhard, Harold E. "Charles Chauncy: Colonial Liberal, 1705–1787." Unpublished Ph.D. dissertation, University of Chicago, 1945.

Brooks, Christopher. "An Intellectual Biography of Charles Chauncy." Unpublished B.A. thesis, Princeton University, 1970.

Counts, Martha L. "The Political Views of the Eighteenth Century New England Clergy as Expressed in Their Election Sermons." Unpublished Ph.D. dissertation, Columbia University, 1956.

Dewey, Edward H. "Charles Chauncy." Ms. thesis, Harvard University Archives, 1931.

Gibbs, Norman B. "The Problem of Revelation and Reason in the Thought of Charles Chauncy." Unpublished Ph.D. dissertation, Duke University, 1953.

Griffin, Edward M. "A Biography of Charles Chauncy (1705–1787)." Unpublished Ph.D. dissertation, Stanford University, 1966.

Jones, Barney L. "Charles Chauncy and the Great Awakening in New England." Unpublished Ph.D. dissertation, Duke University, 1958.

Lippy, Charles H. "Seasonable Revolutionary: Charles Chauncy and the Ideology of Liberty." Unpublished Ph.D. dissertation, Princeton University, 1972.

Weiner, Sylvan R. "Charles Chauncy and the Great Awakening." Unpublished B.A. thesis, Harvard College, 1953.

Index